Birth Space, Safe Place

Emotional Well-Being through Pregnancy and Birth

Adela Stockton

 FINDHORN PRESS

Published in 2009 by Findhorn Press, Scotland

ISBN 978-1-84409-165-2

Edited by Jean Semrau
Cover Art by Marlene L'Abbe © Water Spider Designs, 2004
Cover design by Thierry Bogliolo
Interior design by Damian Keenan

Printed and bound in the European Union

1 2 3 4 5 6 7 8 9 10 11 12 14 13 12 11 10 09

Published by
Findhorn Press
305a The Park, Findhorn
Forres IV36 3TE
Scotland, UK

Telephone
+44-(0)1309-690582
Fax
+44-(0)131-777-2177

info@findhornpress.com
www.findhornpress.com

"Daring to live means

daring to die at any moment

but also means daring to be born,

crossing great stages of life in which

the person we have been dies,

and is replaced by another

with a renewed vision of the world,

and at the same time realizing that

there will be many obstacles

to overcome before we reach

the final state of Enlightenment."

ARNAUD DESJARDINS [1]

Contents

Introduction

*"We need nothing less than a revolution
in our attitudes towards conception,
pregnancy, birth and parenting."*
SOPHIE STYLE [1]

The idea that protecting normality in childbirth is essential to the long-term health of humanity lies at the heart of this book. If, as I believe, our emotional and spiritual wellbeing has a direct bearing on our physical health, it makes sense that accessing emotional support through pregnancy, birth and early parenting days can help women stay healthy in mind, body and spirit during this life-changing time. However, while we may know that having a stress-free pregnancy and gentle birth is important for the future health of both mother and baby, more often it is the commitment to making this happen for ourselves – frequently amidst a shortfall of supportive services – that is the real issue.

This book is therefore intended as a companion, an accessible guide to your emotional journey through pregnancy and birth. I hope that it supports you in clearing the past as best you can to prepare the way for an unhindered labour, and accompanies you through to a positive birth experience and joyful meeting with your new baby. Focusing on the wide spectrum of feelings that may arise for you as your baby grows within, as you face the choices that form an essential part of your journey to parenthood and as you adjust to your new role as a mother, I hope that it gives you confidence to explore emotions that you may otherwise find difficult to share. With its practical suggestions and resources for laying fears to rest, keeping birth gentle and protecting your baby-moon (see Glossary), I hope that it shares your rite of passage to becoming a mother with positive affirmation. Overall I trust that the words and imagery of this book will encourage you to embrace the spiritual journey of birth, reminding you that you are in control of your body and that a momentous occasion is indeed taking place as you bring new life into the world.

On homeopathy

I have included suggestions for homeopathic remedies as an integral part of this book. Homeopathy can be a wonderful tool to access during the childbirth year, whether as a first aid measure in the home or constitutionally, under the guidance of a homeopath, to address deeper issues. In contrast to the potential side effects and piecemeal treatment often attributed to orthodox medicine, I have always felt drawn to homeopathy's precise yet subtle action, especially the way it supports human wellbeing so completely at an emotional, as well as physical, level.

I have noticed that an integral part of the homeopathic consultation often involves pregnant women or new mothers voicing their anxieties or making a commitment to personal change in attitude or lifestyle. My feeling is that these intentions come hand in hand with any effects the remedy may have, but it is the gentle support of homeopathy that can help you find the confidence to carry them through.[2] Please see Appendix A for guidelines on taking homeopathic remedies.

On midwives and doulas

The midwife is a professionally trained and qualified clinical practitioner who must be registered with the Nursing and Midwifery Council (NMC) in order to work legally within the UK (see Appendix C for regulation of midwives in the US and Australia). Her role is to provide total care for your physical needs through conception, pregnancy, birth, and up to 28 days postnatal, so long as you and your baby are well. Should you need any medical treatment during this time, she will refer you to the appropriate doctor. Supporting your emotional and spiritual needs normally also forms an integral part of this care. The UK midwife is employed by the National Health Service (NHS) or may work as an Independent Midwife (IM) (see Appendix C for status of midwives in the US and Australia).

In some areas of the UK you may know your NHS midwife well and there may be plenty of time to talk through with her any concerns or specific wishes you have regarding your care. Increasingly, however, she may not be able to give you the personal attention she would like due to lack of resources (staff and time), and may therefore focus more on your physical and clinical checks than on what you have to say or need to know. The IM (see Resources) is chosen and employed specifically by you, providing your care on a wholly individualized basis. As she is able to offer continuous one-to-one clinical and physical guidance through your pregnancy, birth and early parenting days, she can also support your emotional and spiritual needs as a truly integrated part of her service.

The doula (see Resources) is a lay birth or postnatal companion who is usually a mother herself and who may have undertaken a period of preparation to work as a doula, although this is not mandatory. She provides continuous emotional and practical support to mothers, couples and families through pregnancy in preparation for birth, throughout labour and during the first postnatal months. Never offering clinical or medical advice, she can suggest further resources that may help you in making informed choices about your maternity care. Crucially, the doula is chosen and employed by you (and your partner), although some doulas are employed by government schemes to support vulnerable mothers, while others work voluntarily with women in prison. Essentially your doula is someone you know and trust to uphold your philosophy of birth and parenting, to protect your memories of your birth experience and to assist you in your transition to parenthood in the way that is right for you and your partner. She may also help facilitate communications between you and other caregivers.

Although a midwife (or a medical doctor) are the only people legally qualified to take on the responsibility for your *clinical* care during the time around childbirth[3], my feeling lies in accordance with many mothers' testimonies: that so long as you have chosen her with integrity, it matters not whether your key birth *supporter* is your midwife, your doula, your mother, your sister or friend. This support may be in addition to or instead of your partner.

On use of language

The *Oxford English Dictionary* defines the term "normal" to mean "usual, regular, common, typical, average, standard". In the context of birth, "normal" is generally understood as "vaginal", the route by which babies are commonly born, but the term is used *regardless* of whether there has been any medical intervention during labour. Please note that for the purpose of this book, all my references to "normal" are intended to mean "gentle" birth, with no intervention at all – that is, a completely physiological labour and birth with the woman free to move around and take up any position she wishes, without continuous monitoring of the baby's heartbeat, without any artificial means of starting off or speeding up the process, without any drugs for managing pain or the placenta and without an episiotomy.

I would like to add that while, for consistency in reading, I refer to the baby as female and the partner as male throughout the text, I equally respect and honour male babies, midwives and doulas, and female partners.

1

Conscious Conception?

"Pregnancy, birth and motherhood move us
further along on life's continuum.
They challenge us to create a new normality."
PAT THOMAS[1]

As you begin reading this book you may find it useful to take some time out to explore where your understanding and feelings about having a baby originally came from. Perhaps you listened to the birth story of a family member or heard about a friend's experience of birth? Maybe you absorbed the information through observing pregnant women from your local community as they became mothers with new babies? Perhaps you have taken in more through reading books and magazine articles, or watching TV adverts and soap operas? As our physical bodies hold the memory of everything we know or have experienced in our lives, it is likely that you already have deeply rooted expectations of pregnancy and birth. Accessing these thoughts can help you build a picture of what you would like or need to know, now that you are the one who is soon to become a mother, whether for the first or a subsequent time.

Initial impact

For many women, conception is a joyous moment and the pregnancy that follows is a time of conscious celebration; for others, the reality of supporting new life and the lifetime responsibility that accompanies becoming a parent can sometimes seem overwhelming, even when their pregnancy has been planned. Whether you are in or out of a committed relationship, employed or unemployed, in your teens or your forties, at the time you made the choice (anticipated or unanticipated) to become a parent, it is likely that you had an established way of going about your life, upon which the arrival of your baby will almost certainly make a considerable impact.

Yet why is it that some women sail through the beginning of pregnancy on a wave of glorious triumph, anticipating motherhood with a sense of purpose, adapting joyously to the impact of conception, while others can spend the first trimester feeling emotionally low and confused? Within Western culture we are bombarded with images of "perfection" around becoming a parent: that women bloom while they are pregnant, give birth to "perfect" babies and adapt instinctively to the mother role. Such unrealistic images may do little to boost your self-confidence if you are struggling to surrender to the changing needs of your own body during pregnancy. When, having been a normally fit and healthy woman, you feel drained of energy and constantly as if on the point of vomiting, it can be tempting to wish that you had never taken the plunge. Having made a conscious choice with your partner to become pregnant, any sense of guilt that you might feel if you find yourself resenting your baby for causing you to feel so wretched and debilitated may seem utterly unjustifiable. Our "designer-baby" culture expects you to celebrate the creation of new life, particularly if you invited it in.

Katherine's story

I was 38 when I came to the decision to have a baby. For Innes and me, our recognition of each other as soul mates was instant and the love between us quickly sparked an overwhelming desire to have a child together. So we conceived and I sensed the spectacular miracle of a new life beginning deep inside me. We rejoiced that we had been blessed with such opportunity. I anticipated feeling close to and aware of the spirit within my womb for every moment of the ensuing nine months, long before I could feel her actual movements. I imagined protecting her from every possible danger and evil that lurks out there in the real world. I felt a sense of achievement, of becoming a "whole" woman, of having new purpose. I wore the serene smile of she who harbours a wondrous secret within. Innes swaggered slightly as he walked..."I'm going to be a father! Look at my pregnant wife!"

Then the euphoria of the first few weeks waned dramatically as I started to feel nauseated by foods that I had particularly previously enjoyed — wine, garlic, olive oil. I became hypersensitive to smells that I had loved — my perfume and Innes's natural scent. I felt completely exhausted and queasy 24 hours a day. And I did not want to be touched, least of all in an intimate way. Innes, with the best will in the world to support me through all the idiosyncrasies of pregnancy that he had heard of, began to wonder if I was the same woman he had originally made his commitment to, indeed if things would ever go back to "normal" again. Hardest of all, it became such an effort to maintain clear, unconditional communication between the two of us.

A dark cloud of despair and inertia engulfed me. I could not work, I could not play. I felt trapped by the inevitability of having chosen this path in life and its implications, overwhelmed by the responsibility it entailed, all compounded by a terrible guilt for feel-

ing this way about something so precious. I certainly realized that I would never truly be "free" again. Innes and I entered a state of grief for the bubble of love and energy that we had existed in from the moment we had met and which appeared at this point to have burst in our faces.

And all because we wanted to have a baby!

Katherine's mood improved almost overnight once her nausea lifted at the beginning of her second trimester, and she went on to enjoy the rest of her pregnancy and a gentle birth. However, she continued to struggle with her loss of freedom well into the early years of her baby's life and chose to work through these issues with the support of a trained counsellor (see Resources).

It is ironic that during the time when you can be feeling at your worst, few people may know that you are pregnant; our society has embraced the twelve-week silence "just in case you have a miscarriage" as the norm. Yet, isn't the instance of suffering a miscarriage exactly when you do need some extra emotional support and empathy, some understanding from your workplace, some gentleness and nurturing while you grieve for the life that has been lost?

While you may be amongst those whose experience of the beginning of pregnancy has been uplifting, if it has not been easy and fallen far below your expectations there may be some solace in knowing that you are not alone: for a great many women this is a normal part of the childbirth process. You may find it helpful to confide in another pregnant woman or recent new parent, friend or sister to share your grumbles, but without shutting your partner out; you are nurturing his child, too, and he can share in your experience even if it is difficult for him to relate to how you are feeling.

Pregnancy nausea

Your baby is an entire individual, separate from you in mind, body and spirit from the point of conception, even though she is dependent on you for nourishment and nurturing for the best part of nine months. Various theories about "morning sickness" suggest that it may be caused by the combined emotional and physical process of your body coming to terms with your baby's presence as she establishes herself in your womb. It is not unusual for women to have fears around becoming a mother for the first time, or to be holding unresolved issues from a previous pregnancy or birth, whether spoken or unspoken, which may contribute to this initial conflict – a good example of how our emotions can affect our physical body.

Patrick Houser, co-founder of the Fathers-To-Be network, writes of how his wife worked through her pregnancy nausea after they conceived their second child using affirmations.[2] She wrote down a list of affirming statements about her new pregnancy and focused on her intuitive response to each of them. Although consciously she was happy to be pregnant again, she discovered some inner hesitation due to her fear of suffering another traumatic birth experience as with her first baby. By repeating her affirmations on a daily basis, she was able to reassure herself and change the dynamic of her feelings so that the conflict within her body, and subsequently the nausea, subsided. This took only four days.

You may also find that the following homeopathic remedies help you during this time. Simply suck one tablet as symptoms arise (see also Appendix A).

ARSENICUM 30C - You may feel anxious and restless. You vomit frequently, feeling worse – faint and sweaty – afterwards. Warmth and warm drinks make you feel better.

NUX VOMICA 30C - You may feel irritable, angry and hypersensitive to noise and smells. Vomiting is difficult but makes you feel better. You feel worse immediately after eating and from tobacco smoke.

PULSATILLA 30C - Your emotions are up and down, happy one moment, weepy the next, and you feel more in need of support than usual. Vomiting makes you feel worse. Fresh air and cold drinks make you feel better, you desire sour refreshing foods and drinks.

SEPIA 30C - You may feel indifferent and unenthusiastic about things and people you normally enjoy. You experience an empty feeling in your stomach, particularly around mid-morning. Eating and taking vigorous exercise such as dancing makes you feel better. You crave vinegary foods.

Focusing within

It is important for your self-esteem as an expectant mother and for the wellbeing of your baby to keep talking to her. By explaining that you are suffering due to some of the normal physical discomforts and life changes of pregnancy, you can reassure your baby that you still love and cherish her and that your feeling low is not a rejection of her. This honesty of communication forms the basis for a positive way forward in building your parent-child relationship with the clean energy of clarity, avoiding the insidious negativity of guilt, a healthier option for both you and the future generation.

Try to listen to your inner needs: to rest when your body asks you to, to eat and drink whenever you feel like it. Choose slow energy release foods such as oats and pulses, healthy options such as wholemeal bread and wholegrain cereals, plenty of fresh fruit, salad and vegetables, herbal teas and filtered water, avoiding as far as possible sweet drinks and processed foods that are high in sugar and salt. You may like to consider regularly adding organic alfalfa to your salads as it is rich in iron and calcium and contains Vitamin K; it is easy to grow your own from seed in a jam jar. Try also to take in some daily fresh air and regular exercise, which can be as simple as a walk in the park or countryside, and approach one day at a time.

It is a strange phenomenon but you may find that it is your partner rather than you who is suffering from the symptoms of pregnancy! And for a few women, your pregnancy nausea may continue all the way through until your baby is ready to be born. Whatever your experience, I would encourage you to simply find the way that feels right for you to reach your second trimester when, for the vast majority of women (or partners), your energy and verve will improve.

2

Clearing
the Past

"Healing means listening to the lost voice of your soul...
Take responsibility for your healing process.
Take your health and wellbeing into your own hands."
BENIG MAUGER[1]

The idea of clearing out the old to make way for the new will most
likely be familiar to you and in an ideal world we might all choose
to make peace with difficult past experiences before even conceiving our babies.

I have noticed, as natural birth pioneer Michel Odent also
suggests,[2] that women often give birth in the same way that they
were born themselves. This means that at some level of consciousness we may be remembering our own birth while giving
birth to our own baby. Having an awareness of this carries huge
potential for the healing of any of our own personal birth trauma
that might still be lingering. Sometimes simply acknowledging
memories that surface, whether spontaneously or during a thera-
peutic session, can be enough to help you move through the fear
and avoid needing to repeat the same pattern during the birth of
your own baby.

Callie's story

During my last cranial session, while she (therapist) was working on me, she asked me if I had been born with the cord round my neck. In that instant I not only had a – literally – choking sensation in my own throat, but I also vividly recalled the terror and panic I had felt when they told me that Ella (daughter) had the cord round her neck when she was born.

Suddenly it all seemed clear, why I thought she might die – because that was how I had felt when I was born (that I might die). Yet now I feel like I can let it go, and I hope that will help Ella in some way to process her experience of it, too.

By laying as many ghosts to rest as you can during the course of your pregnancy, before your baby is born, you give yourself the opportunity to resolve former issues that could re-present themselves during your labour, creating barriers to a normal birth. At the same time you will be preparing for your new baby as an individual in her own right, setting a precedent for you both to go forward without holding on to the past.

Loss and bereavement

Many mothers will sadly suffer a miscarriage before giving birth to their first baby, or between pregnancies. Such loss of life is a painful experience and rather than allowing yourself to feel the pain, the first reaction that you and your partner may have is to try again to conceive. If you can, however, it is important to permit yourself the time to acknowledge and grieve for the life that has been lost before rushing into another pregnancy. All the expectations and disappointments you have carried for your lost baby can become transferred onto the new life you create, hindering rather than supporting your new baby as an individual being. This can also be the case where you have decided, for whatever reason, to terminate a pregnancy, or where you have suffered a stillbirth or your baby has died a short while after birth.

If you have not done so already, you may find it helpful to create some way of celebrating the life of your baby who died. For example, you may like to take a few hours out from your normal day, find a peaceful place either alone or with your partner and/or any significant other(s), light a candle and simply say all the things you ever wanted to say to the baby you have lost. This kind of ceremony can allow your feelings of sadness and anger to release in a safe place, and you can complete the ritual with a particular thought or reading, so that as you blow out the candle you know that your baby's spirit is free, but that she will never be forgotten. Some parents find it helpful to plant a tree or a flowering shrub in memory of their baby, again acknowledging her spirit but letting her rest in peace.

You can take the homeopathic remedy Ignatia 30c once a day for a few days following your loss, to help with processing your immediate grief. Try to give yourself some time off work or some extra childcare support and be gentle to yourself, allow yourself the space to cry. You may find that it becomes hard to communicate with your partner as you each grieve in your own way, but try to let each other know that your paths of communication are not indefinitely closed, and if possible spend some time alone with each other, doing some of the things that you both enjoy as a couple. You may also choose to contact the Miscarriages Association or the Stillbirth and Neonatal Death Society (SANDS) who offer bereavement support after the loss of a baby (see Resources). If you have suffered frequent miscarriage, it can be worthwhile consulting a homeopath for more individual treatment (see Resources).

Homeopathic case study 1

Katie came to see me at 36 weeks through her fourth pregnancy, initially because her baby was lying in the breech position (see Glossary). She had however suffered two miscarriages since her first child was born. Still desperately grieving for the babies she had lost and, although aware of the effect this might be having on the baby she was carrying, she felt emotionally stuck and unable to move on. She very much wanted to clear the way for a gentle birth with her current baby, and was aware of how her grief might block the birth process. We talked about ways of honouring the short lives of her lost babies and accepting their right to rest in peace, thereby opening the opportunity to give herself permission to celebrate her current pregnancy. She went home with two doses of Pulsatilla (as a constitutional remedy) and the promise to spend some quiet time with herself and her unborn baby every day, gently working at resolving her grief and reassuring this baby that she was looking forward to her arrival. Her baby turned into a head down position without the need for the second dose of Pulsatilla and Katie went on to enjoy a gentle, fulfilling birth experience.

N.B. While Pulsatilla has a reputation for being "the" homeopathic remedy for encouraging breech babies to turn, in my experience I have only witnessed such success when it has also been indicated as the mother's constitutional remedy.[3]

Difficult previous birth experience

It is possible that you are feeling apprehensive about having your next baby due to having suffered a negative experience with the birth of your last. Sadly, there is an abundance of "bad birth" stories at large as women increasingly speak of the emotional and/or physical trauma that they suffered during childbirth. Many report feeling that an assumption had been made by their caregivers that as long as their baby was "healthy", it did not matter how she was born. While sometimes the physical safety of a baby at the time of birth can become a priority and require medical intervention, this does not need to be at the expense of the emotional needs of the mother, father or family. Some new mothers have been severely emotionally scarred by the lack of provision of appropriate care during the time around their baby's birth.

Deidre's story

My baby was breech and although I really, really wanted to have a normal birth, the consultant waved his hand in the air and said, "Do you want your baby to die?" and gave me a date to go in for caesarean. I was too frightened to refuse. It was awful, not the birth I had hoped for at all, and afterwards I got depressed which I'm sure was because I couldn't have her naturally.

Due to the emotional pain of her previous experience, Deidre was unable to enjoy much of her second pregnancy for fear of it ending in another caesarean birth followed by a further bout of postnatal depression. However, towards the start of her third trimester she decided to employ a doula for additional personal support, with whom she was able to work through much of her sadness and anxieties prior to labour. She then went on to have a normal, gentle birth.

Certainly, many women who have had a caesarean birth the first time around go on to enjoy a physiological birth with their next or subsequent babies, which can be a powerfully healing process in itself. Exploring with your midwife or doula at which point in your previous labour your caesarean occurred, and why, can be key to helping you to emotionally as well as physically cross that same threshold during your labour this time round. You may also like to create some affirmations to help restore your faith in your body to give birth vaginally. The Association for Improvement of Maternity Services (AIMS) publish a useful booklet on vaginal birth after caesarean (VBAC) (see Further Reading, Resources).

Any kind of interventional birth can be traumatic, however, for both mother and baby, and if you are currently in the throes of conceiving another baby or are already newly pregnant after a previous difficult experience, now might be the right moment to seek out some additional support while you clear the way for this new life. The value of open communication with your partner throughout this process is paramount as ever; he is likely to have his own painful memories and anxieties, too, but sometimes it can be hard for couples to be objective together. Talking your experiences through with someone you feel you can trust, who is specially designated and less emotionally involved, such as your midwife, doula or a trained counsellor, can be useful in assisting you (both) to lay some ghosts to rest and move forward in a positive way. It is possible to access your maternity notes from your last birth to which you can refer during the debriefing (see Glossary) session if you wish; you will need to contact the Head of Midwifery at the maternity unit where you gave birth for help with this. You may also choose to access telephone support through Sheila Kitzinger's Birth Crisis Network or the Birth Trauma Association helpline (see Resources).

Another useful and non-confrontational way of releasing both physical and emotional trauma can be to visit a cranial osteopath (see Resources) for gentle rebalancing treatment. Some practitioners will work on the child with whom you shared the previous traumatic birth experience at the same time. Thinking about setting up some additional support for you and your partner during labour this time around, such as taking on a doula to help protect

your birth environment from fear and disturbance, or planning a
homebirth (see Further Reading, Resources) with an independent
midwife might also be useful in re-building your confidence towards a more positive birth experience.

Issues of abuse

If you are aware of having suffered any physical, emotional or sexual abuse during your life, you may find it valuable to try to process
some of the issues with a trained counsellor (see Resources) before becoming pregnant. An experienced practitioner can support
you in an unconditional way, providing a safe place for you to express strong emotions if you need to, and ensuring that you bring
some closure to the way you are feeling at the end of each session.
Sometimes just talking things through with a third party can be
enough to clarify your thoughts and allow you to forgive and move
on; sometimes more work is necessary. A skilled counsellor can
facilitate your often painful and difficult journey through the issues at your own pace, in a way that feels safe for you, and in a
way that friends or family perhaps are not so able because of being
more emotionally involved with you. Homeopathic remedies can
also be invaluable in supporting you through this time, although
here it is advisable to seek out a homeopath who will be able to
prescribe your medicine on an individual basis (see Resources).

Memories of abusive events can be triggered again during labour with traumatic impact, especially by internal examinations
or by the sensation of the birth process itself. Even if you do not
feel ready or able to process any of your experiences at this time in
your life, you may feel able to trust one of your caregivers enough
to disclose what has happened to you, so that she can take care
to be particularly sensitive to your needs and support you to feel
safe and in control at all times. I would encourage you to follow

your instincts on whom to trust. While some women feel that they have not always been listened to by their NHS midwife and would have preferred to have chosen someone with whom they had already made an established relationship, such as a doula or independent midwife, others have received excellent support from their NHS midwife. Whatever feels right for you, a positive birth can sometimes lead to empowering you towards processing and letting go of some of your trauma, helping you heal and enjoy life with your new baby.

Sara's story

I had been raped by my brother and was terrified that it would all come back to me during labour. I didn't want that, for me or my baby. But the midwives were great. As soon as I told them what had happened, they were just there for me, explaining everything that was happening and what was going to happen next so I could keep focused and not let any memories in. I needed an epidural and in the end he was forceps, but it was OK, my midwife stayed right beside me talking me through it. It made me feel like I had won, I had my baby, I didn't freak out or lose control. I felt strong.

For some women, disclosing information to their partners about previous abuse is unthinkable, or in other cases, sharing such distressing memories has served to alienate the relationship rather than drawing the couple closer together. In Sara's case, however, her partner was aware of her painful history and had been consistently involved in supporting her to come to terms with it.

Debra Pascali Bonaro, American doula and childbirth educator, documents eleven inspiring birth stories in her film *Orgasmic Birth*[4]; perhaps the most powerful is that of the mother who is a sexual abuse survivor. At certain points during her courageous birth journey, this woman movingly shares with her attendants how the abuse she suffered is impacting emotionally and physically on her present experience of labour. Most poignantly, we then witness the moment that she realizes she is crossing the boundary from victim to victor, as she actively rises to the challenge of second stage and goes on to give birth, triumphantly. Well supported in her own home by her partner, midwife and doula, the atmosphere remains consistently gentle and safe throughout, and the new mother rests finally in the arms of her partner with their new baby – a woman reborn.

One-to-one support

For mothers and couples who have suffered in any of the ways mentioned within this chapter, accessing sustained emotional and physical support from a known confidante during your subsequent pregnancy, labour and birth can make a real difference towards determining a positive and empowering experience. You may be interested to read testimonies of this in David Vernon's remarkable collection of birth stories, *Having a Great Birth in Australia*.[5]

3

Decisions, Choices and Wellbeing

"When harmlessness is your basis for every action,
you will create a birth for
your baby that does not need to be healed."
SUNNI KARLL[1]

Every decision to be made during your pregnancy is yours to make. You are always entitled to ask for and pursue the care that you feel is right for you. If at any point you do not have all the facts with which to make a fully informed choice, you can take more time to find out further information before making your final decision.

From as early on as your first appointment with your midwife, you will be asked to make decisions about important issues such as where you would like to give birth and which antenatal screening tests you wish to accept. These are details that require careful consideration, with your partner, in your own time. If you are happy to accept all that is routinely available, it is your option to do so, but it is also worth noting that just because a test, a procedure or a drug is offered, it does not mean you are obliged to accept it or indeed that it is right for you.

If your wishes are different from the routinely offered options, many midwives and obstetricians will still be happy to support your individualized care; but for some pregnant women, the sense that you are having to fight your corner in order for your needs to be met may have already become apparent. This can be a tiring, undermining and disappointing experience coming at a time when you need positive input towards your plans, and you may find yourself agreeing to protocols that you would prefer to avoid, simply to keep the peace. Women regularly report going along with routine procedures in fear of being labelled a troublemaker and suffering substandard care as a result. Yet policies are only guidelines, not set in law. Unwilling compromise around this most personal and significant experience of your life can stay with you forever and, in the immediate future, may pave the way for a disempowering birth or early parenting experience.

Place of birth

A common area of conflict can arise when you have stated that you would like to have your baby at home. Perhaps your GP says he/she will not support you, or your midwife has warned you that due to staff shortages there will no midwives available to attend you at home. Some mothers even report being told that they are putting their baby at risk by choosing a home-birth. So you may feel obliged, or worse still, frightened into agreeing to go to hospital.

These excuses are myths, however. The responsibility for staffing lies with the Head of Midwifery at your local maternity unit and she is bound to send a midwife out to attend your homebirth if this is what you have planned. She will also organize any emergency medical back up support at home, should the unlikely need arise, so it is not a requirement for you to have your GP's support. A significant reason for a midwife's presence at a homebirth is to continuously monitor and assess your birth process (as in hospital); should she have any concerns for your or your baby's wellbeing during labour, she will request your permission to transfer you to hospital for specialist medical care as necessary.

We know that your birth environment and the people you invite into it can have a huge impact on the way you labour and give birth, both positively and negatively.[2] While some mothers are happy to gather a throng of trusted, usually female family members around them during labour, plus their partner, the midwife and a doula, others choose to have an unassisted or free birth (without an attending midwife) in total privacy, because they do not have confidence in the available maternity services to effectively support an undisturbed birth. Sometimes it may be necessary for you or your baby to need medical treatment during labour or immediately after birth – particularly if either of you has an underlying medical condition – but even mothers who have had a previous caesarean birth for physiological rather than pathological reasons are now beginning to opt for a VBAC (see Glossary) at home. This may not necessarily be because they have been offered this choice, but rather because this is what they feel is right for them and where they feel they have the best chance of experiencing a gentle birth this time around.

Should you find that your partner is feeling anxious or uncomfortable about the idea of you having your baby at home, why not drop in on your local Homebirth Support group together? This can be a useful, non-confrontational way to dispel myths and gain evidence-based facts about homebirth, as well as link up with like-minded parents – all of which may boost your partner's confidence to support you. In the event that you are being met with resistance from your maternity services about homebirth, or any other aspect of your care, try to take your partner, and/or a trusted friend or relative who is fully versed in your wishes and the reasons behind them, to your antenatal visits for moral support. If you have decided to employ a doula, she will be happy to accompany you and support you in expressing your needs clearly. You can also get practical and effective support in securing your homebirth choice by contacting AIMS (see Resources).

Regardless of the normal birth rate statistics at your local maternity unit, home may not, in any event, feel like the right place for you, or your partner, to be having your baby. It may be that you know you will only relax and feel safe if you are in a hospital environment, and that this therefore is the right choice for you. If you would ideally prefer to avoid a large busy teaching hospital, however, you may find there is a midwifery-led birthing centre, offering a low-tech home-like setting and midwife-only care, situated either alongside your main maternity hospital or as a stand-alone unit elsewhere within your local area.

Overall, I would encourage you to consider carefully where you feel safest, and with whom, before choosing where to give birth. Remember, you can always change your mind nearer the time that your baby is due to be born.

Ella's story

I swithered and swithered, from following my head which said "What if the same thing happens as last time and we need to be in hospital?" and my heart, which was overwhelmingly telling me to stay at home. At 37 weeks the midwife started suggesting it might be "too late" to have my homebirth if I didn't decide then. So I did, and even though I ended up needing forceps again for his birth, being able to labour in the peace and privacy of our own home was the best thing, for me and for Thomas (husband). It was so different this time around, no rush, no fuss; even when we were transferred to hospital, I felt so much more respected and in control of the way things happened.

Antenatal screening

In the absence of any family history of genetic disorder or chronically poor health on your or your partner's behalf, considering the implications of accepting a screening test that could end in the termination of your pregnancy is an intensely personal thing and can end up being an emotional rollercoaster. Whether a blood test or an ultrasound scan (USS), none of the tests are 100% accurate and some only give you a "risk factor" which can leave you feeling more confused than you did before you took the test.

Fran's story

The only option my husband and I chose was the 20 week scan. However, the night before we were due to go we had a talk: we found out that we both felt that if our baby had a condition that was incompatible with life, we would prefer for her to die in the womb or shortly after birth without any surgical intervention, than to terminate the pregnancy. We decided that if she had a disability that was compatible with life, that she should be given the chance to be born and live out her natural life, and therefore we felt we did not need to know about it during the pregnancy. The next morning we cancelled the scan appointment with a real sense that we had made the right decision for us.

It is important to spend some time discussing your feelings with your partner so that you are both clear about where you are coming from. Although some parents will feel quite clearly that you need to know if there is any risk at all of your baby having a genetic disorder, so that you can either terminate the pregnancy or plan ahead to care for a child with a disability, others will know categorically that you do not need such information as you would not consider terminating your pregnancy under any circumstances.

This may seem a cold point of view but it is the reality of antenatal screening, and before you make any decision on the uptake of a test, it is vital that clear evidence-based information and counselling is made available to you. If you are not sure that you have all the facts you need with which to make an informed choice, it is absolutely acceptable to request further counselling from your own or another midwife, obstetrician or paediatrician. In this way you can each relieve yourself of any heartache or regret that you may have made the wrong decision, either for you or your partner.

Whatever the issue is, unless you are really in an emergency situation, you can go home and take your time to consider it rather than rush into any decision, and you can even change your mind at the last minute.

Health and wellbeing

The beginning of your second trimester is a good time to think about taking up a weekly pregnancy exercise class such as yoga, dance or aquanatal (see Resources). These activities can help reduce stress, improve your circulation, digestion and elimination processes, and gently build up your stamina: many women report sleeping exceptionally well the night after a class. The exercises also help you to feel more in touch with your body, to become more aware of your breath and the effect it can have on the way you hold on to or release tension – tools that will be invaluable to you during labour. Part of the session is often dedicated to practising relaxation techniques and your facilitator is likely to be a good source of knowledge about other useful resources available to you locally.

Different from classes that specifically focus on preparing for birth (see Chapter 4), these groups can also provide an informal way to meet other mothers-to-be in your area, women with whom you may bond in a lasting friendship as you go on to share early parenting days together. Within gatherings of mothers however, there are always those keen to share dramatic birth stories with you. Try to avoid getting drawn into any "bad birth" tales, for they seed fear and negativity. It is quite reasonable to politely insist that you prefer to dwell only on the positive aspects of this life-changing event that you are soon to experience.

If, along with "morning sickness", you suffered from loss of libido through the early part of your pregnancy, you may find that, as your wellbeing revives during the following months, you enjoy sexual contact with your partner again. It is quite safe to make love while you are pregnant so long as you are comfortable physically as well as emotionally, and it can be a good opportunity to spend some time as a couple together. Your baby may even make it known that she is enjoying the closeness her parents are sharing!

4

Preparing for Labour

"We must attempt to tell the whole truth about birth,
the truth that includes transformation, mastery,
satisfaction, personal power, and the difference
between pain and suffering."
CHERI VAN HOOVER[1]

As the energy of your second trimester begins to wane and as you enter the last lap of your pregnancy, you may begin to feel more tired, noticing the weight of your growing baby, perhaps wishing you had decided to give up work sooner! This slowing-down process paves the way for you to prepare for your journey ahead and can present an opportunity for contemplation on just how you would like your labour and birth to be.

Blessingway

You may consider celebrating your pregnancy and imminent birth by holding a Blessingway during this time. This ancient Native American (Navajo) ceremony was originally held to wish good luck and good health to those embarking upon any particular rite of passage during life. It has more recently been re-interpreted as an opportunity to gather a group of significant women around the expectant mother to celebrate the new life that she is nurturing, and to offer thoughts and tokens that will support her through labour towards a safe and gentle birth. Usually held during the eighth month of pregnancy, it is a powerful way of honouring you and your baby before birth and gathering spiritual support in preparation for the life-changing event soon to take place.

Each ceremony is different according to the mother's wishes and the dynamics of the women attending; you can plan your Blessingway to be just as you would like. You may choose simply to gather together your (usually female) family members and special friends for a meal. Alternatively you may be happy to embrace the symbolic significance of the ceremonial rituals involved (see Further Reading) and prepare the traditional circular candlelit space in which to hold your gathering. In this event, you might include some circle dancing, singing, chanting or meditation during your Blessingway. Some time spent pampering the mother keeps the focus on you in preparation for a smooth journey ahead: someone might brush out your hair while another bathes your feet in warm herb-infused water, others might paint henna patterns on your belly while another massages your hands with sensual oil.

Each guest is invited to bring a symbolic gift, some music, a poem, a song or other creative image, plus one bead. Traditionally, you thread the beads into a bracelet or necklace to keep with you during labour, along with the other offerings, to remind you of all the positive support of your women friends and family. You might also wish to include "weaving the web of yarn" where you start by winding a loop of yarn around your own wrist, then you throw the ball across the circle for someone else to do the same. This continues from woman to woman until a web is woven within the circle, linking everyone together by the loops around their wrists. Each participant then cuts her own loop of yarn from the web and ties it off to form a simple bracelet; this is kept on until everyone receives news that your baby is safely born. Your Blessingway may conclude with a reading or blessing, before you enjoy your final feast which everyone has prepared and contributed to, together.

Whichever way you choose to celebrate your Blessingway, it is important that you are truly able to receive the positive focus of the group during the ceremony. You may therefore like to invite a trusted friend or your doula to lead the Blessingway for you, so that you will be free to participate fully without carrying the responsibility for keeping the dynamic of the group alive.

Preparation for birth classes

Around the beginning of your third trimester you and your partner will be invited to join your local hospital antenatal or parent education classes, even if you are having your baby at home. You may also opt, in addition or as an alternative, to attend an independent preparation for birth class or workshop, depending on what is available in your local area. Often based on established prenatal education philosophies such as Birthing from Within, Active Birth, Lamaze or National Childbirth Trust (NCT), and although still varied in their individual approach, these tend to be more holistically focused and are usually worth the effort if you are keen to keep your birth normal (see Resources). Some classes are offered in six weekly blocks while others are ongoing; the workshops are usually a once-off day or weekend session. The facts and practical techniques that you and your partner glean from these sessions, plus the literature you read and hopefully positive personal accounts that you hear, can help you both feel better informed and more confidently prepared for the birth of your baby.

You might like to start practising the visualisation or relaxation techniques that you learn in your class or workshop more regularly at home around this time. If you are not able to do this without

31

guidance, try taking a little time out for yourself each day, perhaps listening to some soothing music in a warm candlelit bath or enjoying a gentle massage from your partner. These quiet, stress-free moments nurture not only you as the mother-to-be, but also your baby, and finding ways of being able to totally focus in on yourself both physically and emotionally will be useful to you during labour. Please see Appendix B for suggested Relaxation Exercise.

Optimal Fetal Positioning (OFP)

Your 32nd week of pregnancy marks the moment from which to make a commitment to the consistent positioning of your body so as to encourage your baby into an optimum position for labour. New Zealand midwife Jean Sutton's general rule, to avoid your baby settling into a posterior position with her back towards your back, is always to keep your hips higher than your knees.[2] This means that any sort of bucket seat, in the car or at work, is off limits. Try to keep a small firm cushion with you at all times to place under your bottom to raise your hips above your knees, and most importantly resist, if at all possible, the temptation to slump back onto the sofa unless you are lying well over onto your side. You might like to purchase a Birth Ball (see Resources), which is comfortable to sit on as well as ideal for use during labour, and quite fun for toddlers, too! Otherwise, you could try sitting on the floor cross-legged with your bottom raised on a pile of cushions and leaning forward onto the seat of an upright chair, or sitting on an upright chair back to front so that you can rest by leaning forward onto its back.

All this advice may seem more of a nuisance than a support at this stage in your pregnancy, but it is a truly worthwhile way of assisting your baby in preparation for a straightforward birth. A baby who is lying with her back towards your back (posterior) will be less likely to go through the birth process smoothly, your labour will most times take longer, it is likely to feel more painful and therefore poses a higher risk of intervention. Jean Sutton's copious anecdotal evidence suggests that such trauma can usually be avoided if you are prepared to alter your postural habits for the last eight weeks of your pregnancy and on into labour (see Further Reading, Resources).

Breech babies

If your baby is lying in the breech position with her bottom downwards and does not seem keen to turn by the last month of your pregnancy, sticking to all of the above OFP tips as well as crawling around on your hands and knees for ten minutes at either end of the day, or lying with your legs up against the wall with your bottom propped up on two cushions for up to 20 minutes once a day, may still encourage her to turn. Other methods that have a successful reputation include reflexology, cranial osteopathy, acupuncture and moxa sticks (Chinese herbs), but do check that your practitioner has previous experience in treating for breech babies. While it is possible that there may be a physical (not necessarily problematic) reason for your baby lying in the breech, I would also encourage you try to take some time out and allow yourself a careful look at your lifestyle as well. Are there any major emotional stressors that you could eliminate? There is a theory that breech babies are seeking to get nearer to their mother's heartbeat because they are feeling insecure. Are you moving house, campaigning against war, secretly terrified of giving birth? Is there anything you can change, tone down or even stop doing that might be causing your baby undue stress?

A few babies will absolutely refuse to turn and you might therefore decide to start planning for a vaginal breech birth.

Many obstetricians today are reluctant to support this and you may find that you are faced with more decision-making and the undesired prospect of an unprepared-for caesarean birth. Unless you are happy at this point for your baby to be born by caesarean, it is always possible to simply go with your instincts and insist that your baby be born vaginally. Although local hospital protocol will usually require that a doctor is also present or nearby at your birth, it is worth asking your midwife if there are any midwives with vaginal breech birth experience who might be happy to support you at your maternity unit. Failing this, you can contact your Head of Midwifery to request further information and support.

If you are keen to have your baby at home, employing an independent midwife may be your only choice, as some of these practitioners are confident in attending vaginal breech birth. Especially experienced are independent midwives Mary Cronk, Jane Evans and Brenda van de Kooy whom you can contact directly to talk through your intentions and any concerns (see Resources). The AIMS publication on breech birth also contains useful information with supporting evidence to assist you in making an informed choice (see Further Reading, Resources).

"Late" babies

Although normal pregnancy can last up to 42 weeks, or longer for some mothers and babies, most maternity units have adopted a policy for induction of labour at around 41 to 41 and a half weeks. You will probably know that this is a way of starting off your labour by using vaginal pessaries to soften your cervix and set off contractions, often followed by intravenous Syntocinon (see Glossary) to force your womb to keep contracting. More aggressive and therefore more painful than normal labour, induction means you are more likely to request pain medication and as a result of the intervention, more at risk of having a medically-assisted birth.

Fear of litigation and persistent routine-isation of care on the part of medical staff, as well as maternal choice in favour of interventional birth, are major contributors to this culture of artificially speeding up birth. We know that in spontaneous labour babies play a part in starting off the process, choosing, I believe, their time to be born, and it is also said that the *way* a baby is born is imprinted and will reflect the way she goes on to approach life.[3]

What happens then if a baby is hurried through her birth process? With her inner authority, intention and action during her labour journey overruled, her future capacity to establish and maintain her personal boundaries may as a result be impaired, and she is likely to perpetuate her birth imprint by rushing at life. Furthermore, a baby forced out of her mother's body may be born outside her intended astrological constellation: what impact might this have on her overall sense of place and belonging?

If you find your pregnancy lasting longer than 41 weeks and you are under pressure from your caregivers to accept the medical induction that you were keen to avoid, try to set some time aside for yourself in a peaceful, comfortable space and honestly examine how you are feeling about your baby's imminent arrival. You are always entitled to refuse induction if that is what feels right for you, yet perhaps, deep down, there is a part of you that does not truly have confidence in your body to labour effectively without medical help? It is possible that all the stories you have heard about birth have led you to believe this. Or perhaps you are not so much apprehensive about your labour and birth as about how you will cope with a second/third child?

Homeopathic case study 2

*Lucy came to see me at 41 weeks pregnant with her fourth baby.
She was planning a homebirth and was adamant that she was not
going into hospital to be induced as was being suggested by her consultant. She had been experiencing strong Braxton Hicks (practice
contractions) throughout the day and felt that she was on the verge
of going into labour. She was hoping that homeopathy might help
the process along. As we talked I asked if there was anything she
needed to say that might be holding her back. She admitted that she
was feeling rather guilty because she already had three sons and was
secretly hoping that this baby would be a girl, but at the same time
she did not want her baby to feel unwelcome. We explored the idea
of sharing her concerns with her unborn baby openly and honestly,
just as she had expressed them to me. Before she set off for home,
committed to taking some quiet time out to do this, I gave her a dose
of Caulophyllum. She went on to give birth peacefully through the
night at home to a daughter, weighing in at four kilos.*

*N.B. It is a common myth that Caulophyllum is "the" homeo-
pathic remedy to start off labour. In Lucy's case her symptoms fit-
ted the Caulophyllum picture, so it worked well in supporting her
to voice her concerns and let her body move on from hesitant into
established labour. I have, however, witnessed many other cases of
"prolonged'" pregnancy in the light of threatened induction where a
completely different remedy has been required.[4]*

Giving yourself permission to acknowledge any uncomfortable
feelings and discovering a way of making peace with your appre-
hensions can go a long way towards facilitating the surrender of
your body to the forces of nature. If your own gestation was longer than 42 weeks, however, you may find that a similar length of
pregnancy is normal for you and your baby. You can find further

useful information in the AIMS booklet on induction (see Further Reading). It may also be worthwhile knowing that if your baby is, or was, rushed through birth, with the support of a Birth Process practitioner (see Resources), it is possible to create new imprints that serve to transform early trauma, even if this does not happen until later on in your son's or daughter's life.

Birth doulas and birth plan

You may be intending to give birth at home with either an independent midwife or NHS community midwives who you know well, or in a small birth centre where one-to-one care is assured from your midwife. If you feel uncertain that your midwives will confidently support you at your homebirth, however, or if you are planning to give birth in a large centralized hospital where there is a shortage of midwives, you may wish to consider enlisting a birth doula who will provide continuous emotional and practical support exclusively for you and your partner throughout your labour.

It is a good idea to speak to a few local doulas if you can before making your final decision, so give yourself plenty of time to do this by starting your search ideally around 32 weeks through your pregnancy. Choosing someone you instinctively trust or "click with" and who shares your philosophy of birth and parenting is fundamental to your relationship. Your birth doula usually meets with you and your partner several times prior to when your baby is due, offering you an opportunity to talk through any possible previous traumatic birth experience and to learn what your expectations are for this birth so that you can prepare together, focusing specifically on the needs and wishes of you and your partner.

It is certainly worthwhile writing down all your wishes and choices for labour in your birth plan (see Glossary) so that all your care providers can see at a glance what you have planned for the birth of your baby, particularly if you are going to hospital and have not had the opportunity to meet with or speak to them beforehand. This is something your doula can help you with if you wish, and something she can refer to while you are deep in the throes of concentrating on your birth process. While first and foremost at your service, a good doula is also committed to forging positive relationships with your attending midwives so as to avoid any possibility of a disharmonious atmosphere within your birth space.

Your birth doula will stay with you throughout labour, whether at home or in hospital, until after your baby is born. She can help with comfort measures during labour such as assisting you into different positions, laying hot towels across your lower back, offering you frequent sips of water, and, also importantly, supporting your partner to participate in the birth experience in a way that feels comfortable for him. We know that having the sustained emotional support of an additional birth companion who is not part of the hospital system means you are up to 50% less likely to have an unplanned caesarean birth[5] or to ask for pain medication such as an epidural or opiate drugs.[6]

Alternatively, you may be happy to have a female family member or friend who believes in women's innate ability to give birth naturally to support you, while being sensitive to avoid having your partner feel excluded in any way, as his role as the father is a vital component in the greeting of your new baby.

5

Support during Birth

*"It may be worth considering that ultimate
satisfaction with the experience of giving birth
may not be related to lack of pain."*
SARAH BUCKLEY[1]

*"The skill of being with women in pain
in labour often rests in believing in women
when they do not believe in themselves."*
NICKY LEAP[2]

If you had been having your baby during the Middle Ages, you
might have been plied with alcohol and wrapped in herbal poul-
tices or tied to a ladder and shaken vigorously to help you give
birth, but by the 18th century the administration of opiates as
a means of pain "relief" during labour had already become the
norm. Introduction to the concept of breathing and relaxation
techniques during the 1930's therefore proved a radical step forward towards the idea that women were able to participate actively in working with their own labour pain. As to the deeper
emotional and spiritual impact of women's wellbeing during the
time around childbirth, minimal attention seems to have been
paid until the turn of the 21st century.

You will most likely have read or heard about the perceived advantages of the pharmaceutical and interventional forms of pain management that are available to you during labour today. You may feel comfortable with the theory that Entonox (see Glossary), opiate injections and epidurals are safe and effective methods of dulling the pain of childbirth, with allegedly minimal risk to you or your baby. With the disadvantages and side-effects of these methods now documented, however, you may also be well informed of the non-interventional alternatives to working with the pain of labour, such as movement and free positioning, the use of water and birthing pools, aromatherapy massage and sustained one-to-one emotional support. Nonetheless, the realm of what the pain of giving birth will be like and how you will deal with it remains a mystery until you have personally experienced it, and it is this aspect of childbirth that is generally the most feared.

Pain and the "fear factor"

It is perhaps not so much "dealing with the pain" that is the issue, however; it is, I believe, the "fear factor" that is the real concern.

Pain is essential to assessing the progress of labour, it is a positive pain, an objective pain, one that does not last for longer than one minute at a time and one that will end with the birth of your baby. If you are able to embrace the pain without the use of drugs and thereby leave yourself free to move into whatever position you feel you need to be in at any one time, free to consciously engage with the process occurring within your body and not try to fight or control it, free to allow your body to do its work as nature intended, you may well discover a strength of spirit that you never knew you possessed. Yet fear of the unknown, coupled with dramatic stories of birth sagas, can for some women feel overwhelming and disempowering enough to make pain medication seem like the only means of getting through labour. In reality, opiates can distort your perception of the pain, making it harder to work with, even in the event of a normal birth outcome.

How positive your labour and birth experience is, to an extent depends upon the fulfilment of your expectations. If you are able to commence labour without fear, with a positive attitude to the pain, you are more likely to enjoy the journey.

Fear does not always arise from your perspective alone, however; your care providers can also instigate the "fear factor". You may be completely in tune with your body and prepared with an adaptable, achievable birth plan, yet once any hint of doubt or fear about your "progress" on the part of your caregivers surfaces, you will sense it. At a primal level, your brain is set to respond to the first suggestion of an unsafe birthing environment, causing a hormonal reaction whereby either birth is precipitated or adrenalin overrides oxytocin (see Glossary), slowing down your contractions or even bringing them to a halt until you find an alternative space in which to birth safely.

Conversely, as midwife Nicky Leap reminds us, anxiety on the part of your birth attendant may be less due to a perceived problem with your labour, as to her feeling uncomfortable with the way you express your pain.[3] For example, some labouring women find it useful to vocalize loudly when working with the sensation of the contractions but this is not always greeted with approval by the hospital staff. It is possible therefore, that your midwife duly turns your vocalisation into the suggestion that you are not coping well with your labour, offering you pain medication that will inevitably have the effect of dampening your voice.

Morag's story

The midwife said my cervix wasn't fully opened and told me not to push. But I couldn't help it, my body just took over and I was roaring. I never wanted to take Diamorphine (see Glossary) but she said it would help, it was weird, it made me fall asleep between contractions but didn't really take the pain away. I'm sure he (the baby) was slow to feed because of it, though.

With a birth attendant who was not connecting emotionally with her and a husband who was struggling with the intensity of the situation, Morag did not feel supported or safe enough to follow her instincts and confidently refuse pain medication. Indeed the "fear factor" may be less likely to arise when you are at home in familiar surroundings or in a small birthing unit with care from a midwife you know and trust, but in a large hospital setting attended by unfamiliar practitioners, your birth space is not always so effectively protected.

First time labour

If this is your first baby and you have opted to give birth in hospital, it may be useful to understand how routine procedures – for example, internal examinations or policy time restrictions – can potentially disturb your labour. Sometimes protocols may be implemented from a place of fear rather than rationale, and unless you have experienced labour before, you can be unprepared for the extent of their implications. While your midwife is there to support your needs as best she can, if she is not backed up by her senior colleagues, even the most experienced and skilled practitioner can come under pressure from medical staff to intervene if your labour deviates from what is routinely "permitted" in the policy documents.

Clare's story

I was getting on fine in the birthing pool, nice and calm, just me and Chris (partner), my contractions were hard work but not really really sore. Then the midwife came back in and said I wasn't progressing fast enough and that she needed to do an internal and break my waters to speed up my labour. I got out of the pool without questioning it, but then trying to lie on the bed...it was agony. And when she broke my waters my contractions suddenly became so intense...took my breath away... I just lost the plot. If only I had known what would happen (as a result), I would never have agreed to it.

Due to this procedure and its effects on her labour, Clare felt she had no choice but to accept an epidural and then ended up with a forceps birth because her baby became distressed. She had trusted hospital protocol although on reflection she wished she had been better prepared to stay on her own instinctive path. As a novice labourer, provided you and your baby are both well, you may particularly find that you need more flexible time limits in which to give birth gently, in your baby's own time.

Such a phenomenon is poignantly documented in another Orgasmic Birth story.[4] Attended by a confident homebirth midwife and supported by her partner and their doula, this first time mother takes 40 long, hard hours to give birth, yet to a healthy, alert baby in peace and gentleness. It is impossible that such a time span would have been tolerated within a hospital system without medical intervention, yet this is what felt right for this mother, father and baby, and their ultimate sense of achievement is immense.

Furthermore, when the labour process unfolds just as it should, internal examinations to assess "progress" can also be kept to a minimum. For some women these are extremely invasive and uncomfortable; you are always entitled to refuse an internal examination if that is what feels right for you. It is your body and your baby: no clinical procedure can be undertaken without your expressed permission. Alternatively, if sensitively performed when and where you choose by a midwife whom you trust, this examination may provide you with a useful milestone in your labour. It is worth knowing that it is possible for midwives to examine you in positions other than lying on the bed – such as standing, kneeling or on all fours – although some can be reluctant to do this. It is therefore useful to write your wishes around internal examinations clearly in your birth plan.

Being informed and prepared to confidently insist on the care that feels right for you, even despite hospital guidelines, may be one reason to consider enlisting some additional support during labour, for both you and your partner, particularly as a first time mother.

"Cocktail" of hormones

Towards the latter end of the first stage of labour, when your cervix has opened to around seven centimetres onwards and you approach transition (see Glossary), I have noticed that the pace of labour can often change. My feeling is that this is the point at which women acknowledge, whether consciously or not, the need to fully engage with the birth process in order to actually birth their baby. Sometimes, through fear of crossing this threshold, your contractions may slow down, even stop, or alternatively pick up in intensity and suddenly seem overwhelming. It is possible that an inexperienced midwife, or one unaccustomed to attending a labouring woman without an epidural, may not be familiar with how best to support you through this period before your body begins to push instinctively. She may become uncertain or fearful herself and her reaction may be to suggest that you accept medical intervention rather than trusting that focused emotional support might have the same effect.

Australian GP Sarah Buckley describes the delicate and complex balance of hormones that are at work within both mother and baby, and which are essential to maintaining the smooth process of labour.[5, 6] When synthetic oxytocin (Syntocinon) is used to speed up labour, it overrides the natural painkillers or endorphins in your body, making your contractions feel more aggressive. This means you are more likely to feel that you need pain medication, although the disorientating effects of an opiate injection (Pethidine or Diamorphine) or numbness of an epidural may leave you feeling disconnected from your body and from participating in your birth process. While sustained emotional support can make a huge difference here, notoriously this "cascade of intervention" carries a higher risk of you experiencing an interventional birth and often takes its toll on your baby, too, if not during labour then by depressing her instinctive reflexes to crawl, root and suck after birth. Many mothers speak of circumstances such as these that have led to a disempowering birth experience, and some women even report feeling a sense of failure and guilt from having been "unable" to give birth without medical assistance.

If you feel strongly against surrendering control of your labour, I would encourage you to be prepared with a way of maintaining confidence in the power of your convictions, so that you (or your designated advocate) are able to clearly state your needs in order to receive the support and care that is right for you. Being well informed and well supported by those you implicitly trust to uphold your wishes and who are not necessarily part of the hospital system, can be key to minimizing disturbance and safeguarding your chances of experiencing a gentle birth.

Lee's story

I had been in strong labour all night, but by about lunchtime the next day, my contractions slowed right down, in fact pretty much went away. We knew our midwife was under pressure to intervene. Our doula reminded us of what she had suggested during our pre-natal meetings: to ask about the possible benefits, risks and advantages to augmentation, and also what would happen if we refused it. Overall our gut feeling was to do nothing, so we asked our midwife for some time alone to think about it. She was very supportive and once she had left the room, our doula made a nest on the mat with all the pillows and bedding for Kenneth and I to cuddle up in together...then she left us to it! A bit later on I got up to the loo and had one big contraction in the bathroom and then I was off again. She (the baby) was born about an hour later.

Left in privacy this couple instinctively did what they needed to do to help regenerate Lee's contractions. It may also be useful to know that by gently stimulating your nipples you or your partner can encourage the natural release of oxytocin; if you have been lying down for some time, taking a walk around coupled with plenty of close contact with your partner can have the same effect.

The following homeopathic remedies are also worth considering in this situation (or at any other time during labour where the physical or emotional symptoms fit), remembering that usually one dose is all that is needed.

ACONITE 30C - You are extremely fearful, you may say the words, "I am going to die".

CAULLOPHYLLUM 30C - Your contractions have become ineffectual, you feel anxious and exhausted.

46

CIMICIFUGA 30C - Memories of a previous painful (birth?) experience may be resurfacing; you feel emotionally scattered, talking incessantly, switching from one subject to another or expressing great dread of what is to come.

GELSEMIUM 30C - You are afraid of the approaching "ordeal" (anticipatory anxiety). You feel sluggish, your eyes may feel heavy and half-closed, you need to lie down.

KALI-CARB 30C - You experience severe back pain; useful for posterior labours.

KALI-PHOS 30C - You are exhausted, with no energy to keep going. Also useful for birth partners.

PULSATILLA 30C - You feel weepy and clingy like a frightened child, you desire and feel better for fresh air – opening the window or going outside.

An open mind

While giving birth may well be one of the most frightening experiences in your life, it is also potentially one of the most challenging and self-empowering moments you will ever know. Overall, I encourage you to remember that every mother labours differently with every baby, and that every birth holds the potential to unfold in a multitude of different ways. What is important for you and your baby, as well as your partner, is that you feel you are participating in the process through your own volition rather than feeling cajoled, or even coerced, due to your own or someone else's fear. Sometimes, despite all your best efforts, for your baby to be born safely a certain intervention or instrumental birth may become necessary, but when you have been supported in your choices and reached your decisions under your own steam with your needs and wishes respected throughout, you can still experience a positive and empowering birth.

A new doula's reflection

There was no sense of defeat with the epidural because it (the choice) came very strongly from the mother. I learnt that an empowered woman's decision is always the best, no matter what her previous expectation was.

After an exceptionally long, hard latent phase (see Glossary) this first-time mother made a clear choice. Her doula observed how having time out from her labour helped the mother to recover her energy and reconnect with herself, as if she instinctively knew that an epidural at this point was the only way she was going to find the strength to birth her baby. Just two hours later her cervix was fully dilated. Even though, as a result of the way her baby was positioned, she went on to have a ventouse (see Glossary) birth, in retrospect the mother felt confident and proud of the way her birth journey had unfolded, and her baby breastfed with ease.

You may find it useful to read some of the inspiring birth stories contributed by mothers and couples who have worked positively with pain and succeeded in keeping the "fear factor" at bay, in hospital as well as at home, in the AIMS quarterly journals and on the AIMS website (see Resources).

6

The Spirit
of Birth

"...Childbirth in itself is a rite of passage.
Being born is an initiation and giving birth
is a transforming experience."
BENIG MAUGER[1]

The idea that birth is a spiritual journey makes sense in that the process of becoming pregnant, giving birth and entering new motherhood inherently carries the potential for raising consciousness and enhancing spiritual awareness. The moment when the baby emerges from the womb and the woman becomes a mother is still considered a sacred rite of passage within many world cultures where it is honoured in ways that the West has largely forsaken: rituals, ceremonies and songs are used by both labouring women and their attendants in countries around the globe to call for spiritual protection and an easy birth. In the same way that the act of giving birth intrinsically involves the mother-to-be facing and surviving her deepest fears, including the fear of death, it can be compared to meditation and other practices used along the path to spiritual growth. Regardless of denomination, perhaps the Western birthing woman's strongest ally is her faith, her spiritual belief in the emotional and physical powers of her body and in the universe to assist her in delivering her baby safely.

If you have already been fortunate to enjoy, or witness, an un-hindered joyful labour and calm gentle birth, you may agree that it was as if something "other worldly" was occurring. The sense of spiritual strength emanating from a birthing woman in these circumstances is truly awesome. Drawing not only on the power of her physical body but also on the fortitude of her whole soul, she works together with the conscious being that is the child within her, to bring about a safe and non-interventional finale to her labour. As one doula describes, "*It was like watching an angel giving birth.*"

How far you are able, or wish, to engage with this inner journey lies with you as an individual, although, as we have seen, much depends also on the kind of support that is available to you during this time.[2]

Avoiding disturbance

Michel Odent supports the idea that a female confidante, with personal experience of normal birth and trust in women's innate ability to give birth, has a valuable place as an essential caregiver during labour, although he further suggests that the presence of the father-to-be may disturb, even hinder the birth process.[3]

Please take from this what you feel is the right thing for you. Many fathers in today's Western world are happy to be quietly present and involved at the birth of their children, but there are others who do admit to feeling obliged to attend through social expectation rather than choice. For some men, the burden of being your primary emotional support during labour while, as in some cases, the midwife darts in and out of the hospital room to monitor your physical needs, can amount to sheer terror. If you are relying on a reluctant partner's presence in the birthing room, taking on a birth doula may help to allay his load and open a creative space for him to participate on his own terms, leaving you emotionally free to focus on your birth experience.

Well known for his primal health research, Odent also advocates privacy, warmth, low light, no conversation and no strangers as being essential to safe and gentle birth. A bright, noisy, bustling space where you are constantly being invited to comment or answer questions is not conducive to allowing your primal brain to take over from your intellect and facilitate the effective process of labour. If you have chosen to give birth at home, your environment will more naturally be private and free from disturbance. Creating a safe nest-like space in a hospital room may be more of a challenge but with extra pillows, cushions, mats, quilts, some chosen music, essential oils and other personal items that remind you of home and your loved ones, it can be done. A doula's vision in this can be as useful as her extra pair of hands and her guardianship of the door.

Intuition

An integral theme to this book is about encouraging you to follow your intuition, and indeed this forms an essential part of allaying fear and staying in harmony with your birth process. When there is anything that does not "feel right", you are the primary person with the power to act to change the situation. This may not be a conscious realisation, it may simply mean that your instinct is to take up an alternative position from that which has been suggested, or to follow an opposite plan to that which you intended, in order to perpetuate positive progress. I have noticed, for example, how some labouring mothers with a baby in a posterior position will intuitively lie flat on their backs to push their babies out. However, occasionally it may be that you instinctively sense that all is not well.

Andrea's story

I was so deeply into myself during labour but I knew there was something wrong, that she was stuck, but I couldn't come back to say anything, to communicate what was happening. Maybe if someone had asked me why I thought my labour had stopped, I would have been able to speak about it. I would have been able to tell them what they later found out when she was born by forceps.

Sometimes a similar scenario to this may arise where a mother's idea about keeping her birth experience normal is so fixed that it does not allow for her baby's agenda. If you are not supported in listening to your instincts, you may simply miss your inner knowledge warning you that your baby needs extra assistance from your care providers in order to be born safely. A calm, private environment where you feel safe, nurtured and unobserved, free to be yourself and to do what you need to do at any given moment will greatly enhance your access to your intuition.

Natural remedies

Even if it is the only homeopathic remedy you use, I recommend that you suck one tablet of Arnica 30c every four hours throughout labour and twice a day up to five days after your baby is born, to help with the normal bruising and emotional shock of childbirth or any deeper physical trauma. This can also help your baby to recover in the same way, as she will receive it through your breast milk, or it can be administered in powder form directly onto her tongue, particularly if she has suffered a traumatic instrumental birth. Many women also find the following natural remedies useful:

RESCUE REMEDY (Bach Remedy drops) helps with anticipatory anxiety and emotional shock. Squeeze ten drops into a jug of filtered water and sip continuously throughout labour; take five drops on your tongue immediately following birth. Also useful for partners.

CLARY SAGE (essential oil) encourages the effective action of your womb muscles and opening up of your cervix, not safe during pregnancy, use only during early labour or around "transition". Pour three drops into a basin or sink of hot water for general inhalation, or ask your birth supporters to soak a flannel, terry towel or sanitary pad in the water and squeeze it out to place across your lower abdomen or lower back.

Birthing and greeting your baby

If you are able to keep your pelvis moving freely during labour, and whilst actually giving birth, you facilitate more space for your baby to manoeuvre through the birth passage. Upright, forward-leaning positions such as kneeling are useful, and if you do need to lie down to rest, try to ensure that you lie well over on your side so as to avoid your baby sneaking backwards into a posterior position.

Midwife Ina May Gaskin draws our attention to the "sphincter law", explaining how the cervix is a sphincter in the same way as the rectum and will not work to open up and expel its contents without being afforded some privacy.[4] In order to discourage strangers from entering the birthing room, some couples choose to hang a "Thank you for not disturbing us" notice on the door. A birthing pool can also provide you with greater privacy as well as freedom of movement. It is important that you feel able to instinctively take up any position you choose, especially while actually birthing your baby.

Using your voice to assist in the control of your breath can also be useful: deep low sounds or singing can help keep you grounded, and if chanting plays a part in your everyday life this may come easily. You do not need advice about when or how to push during normal labour; this can be an unwelcome distraction, hindering rather than facilitating the work of your womb at a time when you need all your concentration to allow your body to open up. If you are not in the pool, a warmed flannel or sanitary pad laid against your perineum can be soothing while it is stretching up around your baby's head in those final moments before birth.

You might like to consider how you would like to greet your baby at birth and during the initial moments after she is born. Perhaps it feels instinctive for you (rather than your midwife) to cradle her head in your own hand while she is emerging, gently supporting her onto a soft surface. Should you prefer your partner to do this (instead of or in the absence of a midwife), it is important that he does not attempt to guide her in any way. You know how best to birth your own baby; all he needs to do is gently cup her in his hands as she slides out of your body. Or you may be happy for your midwife to catch your baby. Some mothers choose to pick their baby up immediately at birth, others prefer to do this in their own time or have her picked up first by their partner, or you may be happy to have your baby passed straight into the warmth of your arms by your midwife.

We know that holding your baby close, skin-to-skin for at least the first hour after she is born helps her to bond with her parents and establish early breastfeeding.[5] A baby whose mother has not received any pain medication during labour, and who has not been separated from her mother at birth, will instinctively crawl up her mother's belly rooting for the breast until she finds it, self attach and start sucking, usually within around fifty minutes after birth. Even if you have chosen not to breastfeed, you can both still enjoy the benefits of skin-to-skin contact. Should you be unable to hold or unhappy about holding your baby in this way immediately after she is born, she can enjoy skin-to-skin contact with her father or other parent, or with you at any time later on. Either way, the warmth of another body helps her to regulate her core temperature and breathing pattern, and the familiar sound of a heartbeat is comforting to her. If your baby's birth has been gentle and you have opted for a physiological third stage, this special time before the placenta comes can be one of stillness, gentleness and awe.

Third stage choices

Routinely, an injection of an oxytocic drug (Syntocinon or Syntometrine – see Glossary) in your upper thigh is offered to all women, just as your baby emerges and before her cord is clamped and cut. This is with a view to actively encouraging your womb to contract down quickly, so that your midwife can guide your placenta out within approximately the next five minutes, and theoretically minimizing the risk of heavy bleeding around this time. This is regardless of the kind of birth you have experienced. If you have had a labour or birth where there has been any medical intervention at all, it is generally safer to accept an actively managed third stage; but if you have enjoyed a gentle, normal birth and there is no other indication for you to need medical assistance while you expel your placenta, you may prefer to have a physiological third stage. This means that your midwife will take a hands-off approach, she will not administer any oxytocic drug and therefore should not pull on the cord, she will wait until your womb contracts down and spontaneously lets go of your placenta, usually within around 30 minutes although sometimes longer. She will not sever your baby's cord until the placenta is out, or *at least* until it has stopped pulsating, meaning that your baby benefits from a gentle transition between receiving oxygen via her placenta to breathing in air. A baby whose cord is cut immediately at birth is potentially deprived of 50% of her blood volume which can be shocking to her system just when she needs gentleness and calm.[6]

You may alternatively choose a lotus birth where your baby's cord is never cut and her placenta remains attached until it separates spontaneously at her navel around the third day after birth. Many world cultures believe that babies have a spiritual connection to their placenta: lotus babies are reported to be calm and grounded, allegedly choosing the moment they let go of what has been their life support for the past nine months, rather than having it suddenly severed and disposed of. Shivam Rachana, co-founder of the International College of Spiritual Midwifery, provides some essential reading in her inspiring collection of lotus birth stories from midwives, psychologists and mothers.[7]

Delayed placenta?

The birth of your baby marks the end of your pregnancy and the start of a new era for you as the parent of this son or daughter. Occasionally your placenta may not show any signs of separating or being expelled from your body and, in the absence of any excess blood loss, rather than allowing time and nature to take its course, you may feel under pressure to accept medical intervention. The manual removal of your placenta is undertaken by a doctor (in the UK, although in some countries the midwives will do this) and involves an epidural or spinal block for the pain and a short spell in the operating theatre. Certainly having your baby nuzzling, if not actually feeding, at your breast will encourage the release of oxytocin to help your womb to contract and expel your placenta. However, it may be that you are silently feeling a sense of abandonment as all the focus turns away from you and onto your baby at the point of birth; you may even be feeling that you are not quite ready to let go of being pregnant.

A new doula's reflection

When her placenta showed no signs of coming away, I went and sat on the bed beside her and held her hand, checked she was warm enough and told her how wonderful she was. A moment later she gave a big sigh and her placenta came away. It was as if having the emotional focus brought back to her enabled her to give herself permission to let go and move on.

You may also find the following homeopathic remedies useful, remembering that one dose is often all that is needed:

PULSATILLA - Absence of, or weak contractions; you feel weepy and in need of extra emotional support, you may desire fresh air.

SECALE - You may feel like bearing down, intolerant of a stuffy room. Useful for side effects of Syntometrine (headache, nausea/vomiting).

Whatever your choices for third stage are, it is a good idea to outline them in your birth plan and to check that your midwife is confident in supporting your wishes. This can sometimes be a contentious issue and I highly recommend that you read the AIMS booklet on this subject (see Further Reading) in order to have all the details you need with which to make an informed choice.

Vitamin K – to give or not to give?

This book does not provide the space for discussing this important subject in the detail it warrants, as it is a complicated issue about which you will be required to make a choice based on the information you are offered by the maternity services. There is little evidence to support the routine administration of Vitamin K to all babies, but in order to acquire sufficient information with which to reach your final decision, you will find useful facts in the AIMS publication (see Further Reading). I highly recommend that you make a plan with your partner for your choice well before your baby is due to be born.

7

Early Parenting Joys and Griefs

"It is often difficult for a new mother to recognize her needs and feelings and give herself permission to ask for help. Usually, neither parent has a good understanding of the needs of a young infant and therefore cannot anticipate the endless demands of a newborn child. To shift from an active life where a mother has had social and work contacts with a large number of friendly and supportive associates to meeting the never-ending demand of a young infant is a momentous change. The burden of conscious responsibility with no let up and the unusual and unexpected degree of fatigue can make a mother feel desperate about whether she can survive and how she will manage."

MARSHALL KLAUS, JOHN KENNELL
AND PHYLLIS KLAUS[1]

The time after birth and early days and months of adapting to your new role as a parent can be as intensely special as it can be complicated, whether it is your first, third or fifth baby, and much of it is about discovering what works for you and your family. Many women experience a sense of euphoria during the first few days following birth, fuelling a bout of physical energy that is brought to a standstill as the "baby blues" kick in around day four – when you can weep at the slightest cause or contradiction for 24 hours – and then a gradual settling into the more day-to-day rhythm of life. Every mother's experience is unique, however, and it is possible that it will take you *at least* a fortnight to start finding your feet, if not considerably longer.

The lack of sleep that is a normal part of caring for a new baby will probably make the most striking difference to you, and when you are feeling completely emotionally and physically exhausted, the world can often appear gloomier than it really is. The realisation that you now have a tiny individual human being who is utterly dependent on you for her every need can also prove daunting. Although you may have imagined that becoming a mother would come instinctively to you, and for many women it is indeed a joyful and easy transition, for others the realisation that your life is no longer your own can take its toll in different ways.

It is important to allow yourself to recognize from the outset that every family has different needs; what works for you may differ from the next woman and again from the next. Attempting to fulfil an idea of the "perfect" mother can only prove soul-destroying, as no such person exists. There are no rules – just being there for your baby, for your other children, for your partner and for *yourself* is enough. While the continuum concept (see Further Reading) may feel right for some new mothers, co-sleeping and holding your babe in-arms at all times, others may feel you need some time to yourself now and then – in which case perhaps you can set up another trusted person to look after your baby for a few hours here and there.

Another valuable way to ease yourself into your new role, once you are ready to get out and about, can be to join a postnatal peer support group (see Resources). This provides an informal forum for new mothers and babies to meet up locally, usually on a weekly basis at each other's houses, and it can be a great leveller as you discover that other women are also muddling through the parenting learning curve as best they can. While a few mothers express concerns that postnatal groups may encourage an attitude of competitiveness amongst parents and be de-moralizing rather than confidence building, it is likely that you will quickly get a feel for whether or not the dynamics of your local group seem right for you. Some new mothers find that they continue to meet well into their baby's first or second year, even on through the subsequent births of siblings, forming friendships that become lifelong.

You may feel eager to share your birth experience over and over again, particularly if you feel proud of yourself and pleased with the way things went, and you could find yourself telling more or less anyone who will listen. However, if you are feeling disappointed or disparaged – even traumatized – following a difficult birth experience, you may need to protect yourself from immediate, persistent unhappiness and secure your long-term emotional health by identifying a specific person who can listen to you in a more objective way. This could be your midwife, doula, health visitor or a counsellor, or it may be another mother (or mothers) who has suffered in the same way; alternatively, you may prefer to access support through the Birth Crisis or Birth Trauma Association telephone helpline (see Chapter 2 and Resources).

It is also possible that even if your birth was all that you wished for, the responsibility of caring for a completely dependent human being, along with the impact of the changes that becoming a mother has brought about in your life, fills you with despondency.

Fiona's story

Everything was great, I'd had a quick and easy labour, at home in water just as I had dreamed, and she breastfed with no difficulties. But after about a month I found myself constantly thinking:

"Everything is perfect and I should feel great, so why do I feel so miserable?" I felt like I was suffering a bereavement rather than celebrating new life – it completely did my head in.

Through exploring her feelings with a counsellor on a regular basis, Fiona discovered that the conflict between the joy of the arrival of her daughter and the grief she felt for her former self was a common experience for new mothers, and in time she was able to come to terms with this and settle more comfortably into her new role.

Another factor that can stir up confusing feelings during the postnatal year is if you have had a difficult relationship with your own mother or parents. It perhaps cannot be underestimated how the way we were parented ourselves, especially mothered, can permeate our own way of mothering, particularly with a first baby. We can find our instincts telling us one thing, while our head and deeply engrained early learnt behaviour are telling us something quite different. It is possible that issues which arose between your mother and father, or between yourself and your mother or father when you were an infant, can become transferred unconsciously onto your current situation, causing considerable emotional conflict.

Cara's story

I love Sam so intensely, he has supported me through birth and this first year in every way that I could wish, yet at the same time a voice inside my head keeps saying: "I hate him, I hate him". How can I hate the man I chose to create new life with? It is really confusing.

When Cara was a toddler (at the same stage as her own daughter), Cara's mother and father had split up and she had been surrounded by her mother's feelings of hatred and bitterness towards her father. Memories of this time had been triggered by her own experience of becoming a mother and her feelings towards her partner had become mixed up with how her mother had felt about her father when she was at the same age. Although Cara truly did love her partner, her relationship as a child with her own parents continued to get in the way of her relationship with Sam, until she began to make sense of it after her GP referred her to a counsellor.

More than just "the blues"?

It appears to be a fine line that we tread between the normal ups and downs of the postpartum year and full-blown postnatal illness: many times there is no clear-cut case for medical intervention. Often it is your partner who will seek advice when he has noticed that you are not looking after yourself or relating to your family in a healthy way – although not usually until this has been going on for a considerable length of time. Distress after childbirth can be frightening, whether in the form of clinical depression or post traumatic stress disorder (PTSD – see Glossary), which can include acute anxiety and flashbacks. If you or your partner should sense that your world seems to be racing away from reality, one week, one month or one year after your baby is born, I encourage you not to be afraid to seek out some help.

Although the stigma attributed to postnatal illness still lurks, it is much more commonly talked about and accepted among mothers, new as well as old, as something you can recover from, and embraced by the medical profession as something that is treatable. Your midwife, health visitor or GP are all available (depending on what stage of the postnatal year you are in) to assist you and can refer you to a counsellor, prescribe you medicine, or discuss with you any other options that you wish in order to support your mental health and facilitate your parenting process in a positive way.

You may also choose to consult a homeopath to help you through this time; it is a good idea to find a practitioner who has had some experience in treating women during the childbirth year (see Resources). In addition, you may find it helpful to access a specially designated group such as MAMA (Meet a Mum Association) or the Association for Postnatal Depression for telephone or online support (see Resources). These are but a few examples of possible ways of securing support and working through feelings of unhappiness or distress after birth; they will not suit everyone, and I would encourage you to follow the path that feels instinctively right for you, whichever you choose.

For those of you who manage to ride the rollercoaster of becoming a mother by the seat of your pants and three years later come up for air, thankful to have avoided Prozac yet mindful of how close to the edge you found yourself at times, it can still have been a painful journey. Women who have been level-headed, independent, communicating individuals prior to birth, sometimes find themselves unable to concentrate and irritable with their partners, feeling as if their personality has completely changed. The effect may be devastating and demoralizing, but with Western women today so often completely isolated from any female peer group support at a grassroots level, it is perhaps not surprising that so many new mothers struggle to surrender to the demands of parenting.

Mairi's story

I could never believe how I'd turned into a nagging snivelling shrew, standing weeping on the doorstep waiting for my husband to come home from work so that I could shove our baby into his arms and complain about what a hard day I'd had. I'd even phone him at work and beg him to come home early because I couldn't cope with looking after a tiny baby all day. If only there had been someone around to reassure me, I would have felt less isolated, less afraid of being a "bad mother", less out of control.

This is a common story. Many new mothers live far from their families or the community of women who would have acted as role models and provided emotional and practical support when the baby arrived. There is little doubt that women were never meant to be home alone with a new baby or babies. Accepting this fact may go a long way towards alleviating the guilt that many new parents feel for being "bad mothers" simply because they are isolated.

Nevertheless, the experience of allowing the day to unfold spontaneously according to your baby's needs or learning to slow down to a toddler's pace can offer you the chance to embrace taking a different perspective on life for a while. The time of raising children may be the only time you can admit to yourself that you are a vulnerable human being like anyone else and allow yourself to really feel your emotions – a chance to develop and discover different aspects of yourself. At the same time, extra emotional and practical support during the early days and weeks with your new baby can go a long way towards positive parenting, and for this reason, particularly if you do not have family close by, you may choose to employ a postnatal doula.

Postnatal doulas

Your postnatal doula (who may or may not have been at your baby's birth) will listen to your birth story tirelessly, encourage you to rest and keep well nourished, and support you to feel confident with feeding and caring for your baby. She is not a maternity nurse (whose focus is on caring for your baby) or a nanny or a cleaner. Her role is to facilitate the nurturing of your whole family, just as extended family members still gather round women at the time of childbirth within traditional cultures, so she will usually also help you out with some day-to-day household jobs during your "lying in" period. She can come in for a few hours every day or once a week, in negotiation with what best supports you and your family, and she will usually be available to you until around six to eight weeks after your baby is born. Evidence shows that having the support of a postnatal doula can increase the likelihood of you enjoying established breastfeeding and lower any chances of you suffering postnatal depression.[2] Mothers of twins particularly can benefit from the support of a postnatal doula, not only in view of successful breastfeeding but simply at a practical level, as another pair of hands – such as while gaining confidence in getting out of the house to the shops or on a visit.

Despite the huge adjustment that this life-changing event demands, there is nothing, nothing in the world, like the first time your baby smiles at you or hugs you or tells you that she loves you. There is nothing in the universe like the unconditional love that you receive from a young child. There is plenty of fun and joy and laughter to share as you observe her starting to explore with her eyes, her mouth, her fingers, to experiment with her first words, her first steps. Most parents simply do the best they can, and even if this turns out not to have been ideal, so long as your baby feels safe and loved, you can do no more.

So many mothers speak of the guilt they feel for all the times they got it wrong, but what might seem wrong when compared to another mother's experience may not necessarily have been wrong for you and your baby, your family. I would encourage you to be gentle with yourself and allow yourself to enjoy the time that you have together before she grows and sets off on her own journey into the world; the time is precious and it passes so fast.

Feeding your baby

The evidence that breast milk guards our children from disease as well as protecting their future health in the longer term is well established. In support of this I believe that all babies need to be breastfed as and when they require and that most mothers are able to achieve this. Even against the greatest odds and in spite of appalling socio-economic deprivation, women all over the world are successfully breastfeeding their babies. In countries where artificial milk is not freely available, breastfeeding rates are almost 100%. The "developed" world, however, has distorted the way that women and men view and feel about the human body to such a degree that it has infringed upon the most fundamental of human actions: to provide the nourishment we specifically create for our young. While the option to bottle-feed artificial milk can be essential to the wellbeing of a certain few mothers and babies, there seems no other fundamental justification as to why breastfeeding is not globally accepted as "the way women feed babies". With immediate access to the excellent skills of breastfeeding counsellors if required, I would ask what else is needed to help Western women embrace the decision to exclusively breastfeed on demand?

I therefore encourage you to breastfeed your baby if at all possible for *at least* six weeks. This will give you time to resolve any of the normal discomforts and adjustments that you may face during the early days of breastfeeding, and to reach the point at which many women report starting to really enjoy the experience. You may not know that even if you have had to give permission for your baby to receive artificial milk because you are/were too ill to breastfeed or express your breastmilk, you are physiologically able to start or resume breastfeeding once you are well again, if you wish. Should you be an adoptive mother, you too are able to breastfeed if you choose to do so. You can draw on the support of your midwife or health visitor if that is what feels right for you, but if you find you are struggling with prolonged difficulties, at whatever stage of the postnatal period, it can be a good idea to make contact with a breastfeeding counsellor who will be able to offer you immediate support, information and advice, even over the telephone (see Resources). Once you cross the six-week threshold, however, you may find that you are happy to keep going until six months!

I highly recommend that you explore Suzanne Colson's new mother-centred approach to breastfeeding known as Biological Nurturing, should you be interested to learn more about instinctive behaviour and breastfeeding your baby.[3]

Homeopathy for new mothers and babies

The following homeopathic remedies may be useful during the early weeks following birth, but should you or your baby develop a high fever, it is important that you consult your GP or midwife as well:

ARNICA 30C - For bruising, pain or emotional shock following birth. One tablet per day for up to five days as required. If you are not breastfeeding and your baby needs Arnica, give one powder or granules (6c) per day for up to five days as required.

BELLADONNA 30C - The affected area is red, hot and painful, you may feel feverish. Useful for engorged breasts; suck one tablet as required. N.B. Encouraging your baby to feed on demand means that your milk is cleared regularly from your milk ducts, helping to prevent mastitis. If your baby is fretful and your breasts are full and sore, enjoying some skin to skin contact together in a warm bath can be a soothing way to encourage her to feed. You can also slide one cabbage leaf inside each of your bra cups to ease the discomfort, replacing them as the leaves become floppy.

CALENDULA OR HYPERCAL TINCTURE - Useful for wound healing: perineal tears, stitches or caesarean scars. Pour ten drops into your bath or five drops into a bowl of water or bidet every time you wash.

CHAMOMILLA 6C - powder/granules (Nelson's Teetha is available from most chemists, one box contains several powders in prepared sachets) Useful for teething or colic. Your baby seems angrily inconsolable, one cheek may be red, she is better if she is carried or when driven in the car. Tip one powder onto your baby's tongue as symptoms arise, but do not repeat more than twice in 30 minutes and do not give "just in case".

COLICYNTHIS 6C - powder/granules Another colic remedy: your baby draws her legs up towards her stomach as she cries, she is better with pressure against her stomach such as if you lay her tummy-down over your knee or place her tummy-down over your shoulder. Give one powder as per directions for Chamomilla.

HYPERICUM 30C - If you have a sore coccyx (base of your spine), alternate one tablet per day with your Arnica 30c until symptoms improve.

PULSATILLA 30C - powder/granules Useful for first ear infections and colds with yellow or green mucous, your baby may be weepy and clingy, her mood improves with fresh air. One powder as per directions for Chamomilla.

For more complicated, deeper issues including both physical and emotional effects of birth, it is advisable to contact a homeopath for individual consultation (see Resources).

Cranial-sacral therapy or cranial osteopathy

If you have had an instrumental or caesarean birth it can be greatly valuable to consult either a cranial osteopath or a cranial-sacral therapist for both yourself and your baby as a matter of course as soon as possible after the birth. Even if you have had a normal birth, this can be useful as a means of maintaining good health.

These gentle, non-invasive treatments help you to clear any physical imbalances that can cause symptoms such as headaches, as well as back or hip problems of which you might not be immediately aware but which may resurface at a later date or during a subsequent pregnancy. The sessions can also help your baby to realign and settle from any after-effects of the birth and prevent, as well as cure, symptoms such as colic or sleep difficulties. It is important to find a practitioner who is experienced in working with young babies (see Resources) and, while it is not too late if you do not seek treatment until you or your baby are actually suffering symptoms, it is preferable that your child receives treatment before the age of three.

Immunisation

The decision of whether or not to have your baby immunized is an emotive and personal one. I am often approached by parents who have read the research and have made an informed choice not to immunize, but who are seeking non-invasive ways of supporting their baby's immune system to stay strong and healthy. Although I am able to suggest further resources, support groups and contact with other mothers who have chosen not to immunize, I do encourage all parents to make the choice that they feel comfortable with. If this is to avoid all immunisations, then a homeopath can offer constitutional homeopathic treatment. If the decision is to take some or all immunisations, then homeopathic remedies can help alleviate any side effects. I highly recommend that you research further around this important subject so as to reach the decision that is right for you and your baby (see Further Reading, Resources).

Endnotes and References

FRONTISPIECE

1   From *Buddhist Offerings: 365 Days* by **Danielle and Olivier Föllmi**, © 2003. REPRINTED BY KIND PERMISSION OF THAMES & HUDSON LTD., LONDON.

INTRODUCTION

1   **Style S**, "Womb to World", *Resurgence Magazine: The Heat Is On*, ISSUE 224 (MAY/JUNE 2004), PP. 24-26. www.resurgence.com

2   An edited version of this subsection was first published in *Juno Magazine* ISSUE 13 (WINTER 2007), PP. 42-44, as part of the article "Homeopathy for the Childbirth Year".

3   Nursing and Midwifery Council (NMC) *Free or Unassisted Birthing.* www.nmc-uk.org (ACCESSED 27 AUGUST 2008)

CHAPTER 1

1   **Thomas P**, *Every Woman's Birth Rights* (LONDON: THE WOMEN'S PRESS, 2002).

2   **Houser P**, *Fathers-To-Be Handbook: A roadmap for the transition to fatherhood* (KENT: CREATIVE LIFE SYSTEMS, 2007), PP. 85-87.

CHAPTER 2

1   **Mauger B**, *"Wounded Mothers"*, AIMS Journal VOL. 19:1 (2007), PP. 21-22.

2   **Odent M**, *Primal Health: Understanding the critical period between conception and the first birthday* (FOREST ROW: CLAIRVIEW BOOKS, 2002).

3   An edited version of this case study was first published in *Juno Magazine* ISSUE 13 (WINTER 2007), PP. 42-44, as part of the article "Homeopathy for the Childbirth Year".

4   **Pascali Bonaro D**, *Orgasmic Birth* DVD, 2008. www.orgasmicbirth.com

5   **Vernon D** (Ed.), *Having a Great Birth in Australia* (CANBERRA CITY: AUSTRALIAN COLLEGE OF MIDWIVES, 2005).

CHAPTER 3

1   **Karll S**, *Sacred Birthing: Birthing a New Humanity* (VICTORIA, CANADA: TRAFFORD PUBLISHING, 2003). www.sacredbirthing.com

2   **Kitzinger S**, *Birth Crisis* (LONDON AND NEW YORK: ROUTLEDGE TAYLOR & FRANCIS GROUP, 2006).

CHAPTER 4

1   **van Hoover C**, "Pain and Suffering in Childbirth: A look
    at attitudes, research and history", *Midwifery Today* Issue 55
    (September 2000), pp. 39-42.

2   **Sutton J and Scott P,** *Understanding and Teaching Optimal
    Fetal Positioning,* 2nd rev. ed. (New Zealand: Birth Concepts,
    1996).

3   **Tonetti-Vladimirova E,** *The Limbic Imprint.*
    www.birthintobeing.com (accessed 25 August 2008)

4   An edited version of this case study was first published in
    Juno Magazine Issue 13 (Winter 2007), pp. 42-44, as part of
    the article "Homeopathy for the Childbirth Year".

5   **McGrath SK, PhD, and Kennell JH, MD**, "A Randomized
    Controlled Trial of Continuous Labor Support for Middle-
    Class Couples: Effect on cesarean delivery rates", *Birth* 35:2
    (2008), pp. 92-97.

6   **Hodnett ED, Gates S, Hofmeyr GJ and Sakala C**,
    "Continuous Support for Women during Childbirth",
    Cochrane Review: The Cochrane Library Issue 2 (Chichester:
    John Wiley & Sons, Ltd., 2003).

CHAPTER 5

1   **Buckley S**, "All about Epidurals", *Australian Parents* Issue 106
    (August/September 1998), pp. 43-44.

2   **Leap N**, "No Gain without Pain!" Paper presented at Enriching Midwifery Conference, Australia, March 2000 for Birth International, PO Box 366 Camperdown NSW 1450 www.acegraphics.com.au (ACCESSED 9 DECEMBER 2008)

3   Ibid.

4   **Pascali Bonaro D**, *Orgasmic Birth* DVD, 2008. www.orgasmicbirth.com

5   **Buckley SJ**, "Undisturbed Birth: Nature's hormonal blueprint for safety, ease and ecstasy", *MIDIRS Midwifery Digest* VOL. 14:2 (JUNE 2004), PP. 203-209.

6   **Buckley SJ**, "What Disturbs Birth?" *MIDIRS Midwifery Digest* VOL. 14:3 (SEPTEMBER 2004), PP. 353-359.

CHAPTER 6

1   **Benig Mauger**, *Reclaiming the Spirituality of Birth* (ROCHESTER, VERMONT: HEALING ARTS PRESS, 2000), P.190. The author wishes to thank BENIG MAUGER and INNER TRADITIONS for permission to quote from *Reclaiming the Spirituality of Birth* (2000).

2   An edited version of this subsection was first published in *Birth and Beyond* ISSUE 25 (AUGUST 2005), P. 2, as part of the article "Birth as a Spiritual Journey".

3   **Odent M**, *Birth and Breastfeeding: Rediscovering the needs of women during pregnancy and childbirth*, 2ND ED. (FOREST ROW: CLAIRVIEW BOOKS, 2007).

4   **Gaskin IM**, *Ina May's Guide to Childbirth* (NEW YORK: BANTAM BOOKS, 2003), P. 170.

5   **Righard L and Alade MO**, "Effect of Delivery Room Routines on Success of First Breast-feed," *Lancet* VOL. 339 (1990), PP. 1105-1107.

6   **Buckley SJ**, *Gentle Birth, Gentle Mothering* (BRISBANE: ONE MOON PRESS, 2005), CHAPTER 15.

7   **Rachana S**, Ed., *Lotus Birth* (VICTORIA, AUSTRALIA: GREENWOOD PRESS, 2000).

CHAPTER 7

1   **Klaus MH, Kennell JH and Klaus PH**, *The Doula Book* (CAMBRIDGE, MA: PERSEUS PUBLISHING, 2002), P.169.

2   **Golbert J**, "Postpartum Depression: Bridging the gap between medicalized birth and social support", *International Journal of Childbirth Education* 17:4 (2002), PP. 11-17.

3   **Colson SD, Meek JH and Hawdon JM**, "Optimal Positions for the Release of Primitive Neonatal Reflexes Stimulating Breastfeeding", *Early Human Development* VOL. 84 (2008), PP. 441-449. www.elsevier.com

Appendix A

Taking your homeopathic remedies

~ Avoid touching your remedy – tip one tablet into the cap of the bottle and tip directly into your mouth or pour the powder directly onto your baby's tongue.

~ Suck one tablet under your tongue (do not swallow with water), repeat one dose only if the symptoms persist or reappear.

~ Take the tablet in clean mouth if possible, avoid eating or drinking for 15 minutes either side of taking your remedy (except in emergency).

~ Store your remedies in cool dark place away from strong smells.

~ Try to avoid taking/using any mint/menthol substance or coffee (including decaffeinated) while using homeopathic remedies.

Appendix B

Relaxation exercise (approx. 20 minutes)

You might wish to record this text onto a tape or CD so that you can listen to it at any time.

Find a comfortable position in a place where you know you will not be disturbed. Whether sitting or lying, make sure all your limbs are well supported so that you can completely let go.

Close your eyes and gently become aware of your breath coming and going within your body. Which part of your body does it fill and empty? Does your chest rise up on an in-breath, or your stomach? There is no need to slow down or deepen your breathing, just take care to always breathe in through your nose, although it is fine to breathe out through your nose or your mouth. Give yourself time to become familiar with your normal pattern of breathing.

When you are ready, you can begin to gently direct your breath around your body, encouraging your whole being to relax. Start by imagining you are drawing each in-breath down into your left leg, filling it with fresh air to the tips of your toes. And then, by using your out-breath, allowing your whole limb to empty and softly let go. Repeat this process a few times on the same leg, then slowly move around each of your limbs and other body parts, one by one, doing the same thing, filling and emptying, keeping your breath in a steady rhythm.

Now, feeling your whole body gently resting, soft and relaxed, you may like to go into a space or a place in your imagination that is special to you, somewhere that you feel safe, secure and comfortable. It may be a real place or an imaginary one, somewhere you know well or that you have only seen in a picture or a film, or read about in a book.

Take your time to cast your mind's eye around to see how your special place looks and feels today. What is the light like? Are there any prominent colours or shadows? What do you sense around you?

Can you feel anything against your skin? Perhaps a warm breeze, some soft wrappings, the sun's rays? Can you hear any sounds? Maybe the waves on the shore, the wind in the trees, some birdsong or music?

Do any scents fill the air? Is there anyone with you? You may be quite happy to stay there alone or you may wish to imagine a significant other, person or pet, with you there today.

Over the next few moments, take some time – whatever feels right for you – to focus on your tiny baby in your womb and take the opportunity to share with him or her any thoughts that you need or would like to. Enjoy this quiet time together!

When you are ready, you can begin to prepare to step out of your special place today. Bring your awareness back to your breath again and take two or three deep breaths so as to draw the energy back into your body. Once you have left your safe space, bring your focus back to where you are in actual time and space before gently stretching your body and opening your eyes, and in your own time returning to the physical world. If you are lying down, remember to roll onto your side before sitting up slowly!

You might like to share your experience with your partner and consider ways in which you could both transfer aspects of your special place to your birth environment in order to help you to feel safe and relaxed during your labour.

Appendix C

Midwifery status and regulation in US and Australia versus in the UK

~ Both countries have state regulated (trained, certified) midwives as well as lay (not necessarily trained, unlicensed) midwives – whereas in the UK all practising midwives must be trained and registered. Each American and Australian state has its own midwifery certification body; the UK has only one regulatory body.

~ US Certified Nurse Midwife (hospital, pre-nurse trained)/ Australian Registered Midwife (hospital, mostly pre-nurse trained) loosely equates to a UK NHS-employed midwife (mostly hospital, minimal homebirth, no prerequisite for nurse training).

~ US Certified Midwife (homebirth, non-nurse trained)/ Australian Independent Midwife (homebirth/birth centre, mostly pre-nurse trained) loosely equates to a UK independent midwife (homebirth, no prerequisite for nurse training).

Glossary

First trimester:
from conception until 12 completed weeks of pregnancy

Second trimester:
from 12 to 24 completed weeks of pregnancy

Third trimester:
from 24 to 37 completed weeks of pregnancy

Term:
from 37 to 42 completed weeks of pregnancy

STAGES OF LABOUR

First stage of labour (2 phases):
Latent phase:
from the start of contractions to when your cervix is around 4
centimetres open
Active phase/established labour:
from the start of regular contractions increasing in length
and strength, when your cervix is opening from 4 to 10
centimetres

"Transition":
the period of time between the first and second stage of labour, may last from a few minutes to a few hours.

Second stage of labour:
from when your cervix is 10 centimetres open to when your baby is born

Third stage of labour:
from when your baby is born to when your placenta is delivered complete

MISCELLANEOUS TERMS

Baby-moon:
private, unmeasured time spent with your new baby in a relaxed environment (as defined by Sheila Kitzinger in *The Year After Childbirth*, Prentice Hall & IBD, 1996 p.203)

Birth plan:
a written explanation of how you would like your labour and your baby's birth to be, anything that you wish to avoid or include, etc.

Breech presentation:
a baby who is positioned bottom downwards in your womb

Debriefing:
talking through your experience (of giving birth) after the event

Diamorphine:
> a semi-synthetic opiod for labour – only administered in Scotland; another name for heroin

Entonox:
> 50% nitrous oxide gas and 50% oxygen; called "gas and air"

Oxytocin:
> hormone that is released in large amounts during labour, facilitating birth and breastfeeding

Pethidine:
> an opiate drug, effects less strong than with Diamorphine

Post Traumatic Stress Disorder (PTSD):
> a state of ongoing emotional reaction to the psychological trauma caused by serious threat or actual physical harm

Syntocinon:
> a synthetic form of the hormone oxytocin which makes your womb contract

Syntometrine:
> combination drug containing Syntocinon, which forces your womb to contract, and Ergometrine, which directs blood towards your heart and away from your extremities

VBAC:
> vaginal birth after a caesarean birth

Ventouse:
> vacuum extraction

Further Reading

Approaches to Pregnancy, Birth and Parenting

~ **Buckley S**, *Gentle Birth, Gentle Mothering*, Rev Ed (BERKLEY: CELESTIAL ARTS 2009).

~ **Clarke V**, *Instinctive Birthing* (LONDON: CARROLL & BROWN PUBLISHERS 2005).

~ **Journal of Attachment Parenting International** www.attachmentparenting.org

~ **Juno Magazine** www.junomagazine.com

~ **Leidloff J**, *Continuum Concept: In search of happiness lost* (LONDON: PENGUIN BOOKS 2004).

~ **The Mother Magazine** www.themothermagazine.co.uk

Breastfeeding

~ **Colson S**, "Womb to World: A metabolic perspective", *Midwifery Today* ISSUE 61 (SPRING 2002) PP.12-18. www.midwiferytoday.com (ACCESSED 30 OCTOBER 2008)

~ **Newman J**, "The Importance of Skin-to-Skin Contact (First Feed)", 2005. www.breastfeedingonline.com (ACCESSED 20 OCTOBER 2008)

~ **Robinson VS**, *The Drinks Are on Me: Everything your mother never told you about breastfeeding*, 2nd Ed (CUMBRIA: STARFLOWER PRESS 2008).

Breech

~ **Evans J**, *Breech Birth – What Are My Options?* AIMS, 2005. www.aims.org.uk

~ **Royal College of Midwives**, *"Normal Breech Birth"*. www.rcmnormalbirth.net (ACCESSED 22 OCTOBER 2008)

~ **Waites B**, *Breech Birth* (LONDON: FREE ASSOCIATION BOOKS, 2003).

Doulas

~ **Berg M and Terstad A**, "Swedish Women's Experiences of Doula Support during Childbirth", *Midwifery* VOL 22 (2006), PP. 330-338,

~ **Klaus MH, Kennell JH and Klaus PH**, *The Doula Book* (CAMBRIDGE, MA: PERSEUS PUBLISHING, 2002)

~ **Pascali-Bonaro D and Kroeger M**, "Continuous Female Companionship during Childbirth: A crucial resource in times of stress or calm", *Journal of Midwifery and Women's Health* VOL 49:4 (2004), PP. 19-27.

~ **Schear L**, "Doulas and Daughters", *MIDIRS Midwifery Digest* Vol 17:2 (June 2007), pp. 185-187.

~ **Stockton A**, "Some Thoughts in Response to Lesley Schear's Article, 'Doulas and Daughters' in the June Digest", *MIDIRS Midwifery Digest* Vol 17:3 (Sept 2007), p. 392.

Emotional Support

POSTNATAL ILLNESS

~ **Griebenow JJ**, "Healing the Trauma: Entering motherhood with Posttraumatic Stress Disorder (PTSD)", *Midwifery Today* Issue 80 (Winter 2006). www.midwiferytoday.com (accessed 30/10/08)

~ **Hanzak EA**, *Eyes without Sparkle: A journey through postnatal illness* (Oxford: Radcliffe Publishing Ltd, 2005).

~ **Mauthner N**, *The Darkest Days of My Life: Stories of postpartum depression* (Harvard: Harvard University Press, 2002).

ABUSE SURVIVORS

~ **Simkin P and Klaus P**, *When Survivors Give Birth: Understanding and healing the effects of early sexual abuse on childbearing women* (Seattle: Classic Day Publishing, 2004).

~ **Sperlich M and Seng J**, *Survivor Moms: Women's stories of birthing, mothering and healing after sexual Abuse* (Eugene: Motherbaby Press, 2008).

Finding the Right Care for You

~ **Beech B**, *Am I Allowed?* AIMS, 2003. <u>www.aims.org.uk</u>

~ **Harper B**, *Gentle Birth Choices*, 3rd Ed (ROCHESTER: HEALING ARTS PRESS, 2005).

~ **MIDIRS Midwifery Digest** <u>www.midirs.org.uk</u>

~ **Midwifery Today Journal** <u>www.midwiferytoday.com</u>

~ **Thomas P,** *Every Woman's Birth Rights* (LONDON: THE WOMEN'S PRESS, 2002).

Health and Physical Wellbeing

~ **Balaskas J**, *New Natural Pregnancy* (LONDON: GAIA BOOKS, 1998).

~ **England P and Horowitz R**, *Birthing from Within*, Rev Ed (LONDON: SOUVENIR PRESS, 2007).

Homebirth and Waterbirth

~ **Balaskas J**, *The Water Birth Book* (LONDON: THORSONS, 2004).

~ **Edwards NP**, *Birthing Autonomy: Women's experiences of planning home births* (LONDON AND NEW YORK: ROUTLEDGE, 2005).

~ **Hazard L**, *Fathers Homebirth Handbook* (GLASGOW: SELF-PUBLISHED, 2008). <u>www.homebirthbook.com</u>

~ **Wesson N**, *Home Birth: A practical guide*, 4th Ed (LONDON: PINTER & MARTIN, 2006).

Homeopathy

~ **Moskowitz R**, *Homeopathic Medicines for Pregnancy and Childbirth* (BERKELEY, CA: NORTH ATLANTIC BOOKS, 1992).

~ **Pinto G and Feldman M**, *Homeopathy for Children* (SAFFRON WALDEN: CW DANIEL CO LTD, 2000).

~ **Van Der Zee H**, *Homeopathy for Birth Trauma* (NETHERLANDS: HOMEOLINKS PUBLISHERS, 2007).

Immunisation

~ **Chaitow L**, *Vaccinations and Immunizations: Dangers, delusions and alternatives* (SAFFRON WALDEN: CW DANIEL, 1987).

~ **Gunn T**, *Mass Immunization: A point in question* (KENDAL: CUTTING EDGE PUBLICATIONS, 1992).

"Late" Babies and Induction

~ *"Overdue but desperate for a homebirth?"* www.homebirth.org.uk/overdue.htm (ACCESSED 9 SEPTEMBER 2008)

~ **Royal College of Midwives**, *"Induction"*. www.rcmnormalbirth.net (ACCESSED 22 OCTOBER 2008)

~ **Wickham S**, *Induction: Do I really need it?* AIMS, 2004.
www.aims.org.uk

Optimal Fetal Postioning

~ *"Get Your Baby Lined Up! Optimal Foetal Positioning"*.
www.homebirth.org.uk (ACCESSED 9 SEPTEMBER 2008)

~ *"What's the Big Deal about Posterior?"*
www.spinningbabies.com (ACCESSED 9 SEPTEMBER 2008)

~ **Sutton J**, *Let Birth Be Born Again: Rediscovering and reclaiming our midwifery heritage* (BEDFONT, UK: BIRTH CONCEPTS, 2001).

Spirituality and Blessingway

~ **Corda MVJ**, *Cradle of Heaven: Psychological and spiritual dimensions of conception, pregnancy and birth* (NEW YORK: OMEGA PRESS, 1987).

~ **Cortlund Y, Lucke B and Watelet DM**, *Mother Rising: Blessingway Journey into Motherhood* (HONEOYE, NY: SEEING STONE PRESS, 2004).

~ **Hall J**, *Midwifery, Mind and Spirit* (OXFORD: BOOKS FOR MIDWIVES, 2001).

~ **Karll S**, *Sacred Birthing: Birthing a new humanity* (VICTORIA, BC: TRAFFORD PUBLISHING, 2003). www.sacredbirthing.com

~ **Mauer B**, *Reclaiming the Spirituality of Birth* (ROCHESTER: HEALING ARTS PRESS, 2000).

~ **Resurgence Magazine** www.resurgence.com

Third Stage

~ **Edwards N**, *Delivering Your Placenta: The third stage*. AIMS, 1999. www.aims.org.uk

~ "The Third Stage of Labour: Choosing between active and physiological delivery of the placenta". www.homebirth.org. uk/thirdstage.htm (ACCESSED 22 OCTOBER 2008)

~ **Wickham S**, "The Internal Grandmother". www.withwoman.co.uk (ACCESSED 22 OCTOBER 2008)

VBAC

~ **Lesley J**, *Birth after Caesarean*. AIMS, 2004. www.aims.org.uk

~ **Lowden G and Chippington DD**, "VBAC: On whose terms?" *AIMS Journal* VOL 14:1 (SPRING 2002).

Vitamin K

~ **Hey E**, "Vitamin K: Can we improve on nature?" *MIDIRS Midwifery Digest* 13:1 (MARCH 2003), PP.7-12.

~ **Wickham S**. Vitamin K and the Newborn. AIMS, 2003. www.aims.org.uk

~ **McTaggart L**, Ed. *The Vaccination Bible* (LONDON: WHAT DOCTORS DON'T TELL YOU PRESS, 1998).

Resources

Approaches to Pregnancy, Birth and Parenting Networks

~ **Association for Improvements in the Maternity Services (AIMS)** www.aims.org.uk Helpline 0870-765-1433 (UK) Support and information for parents and practitioners: journal, articles, booklets, campaigns

~ **Association for Prenatal and Perinatal Psychology and Health (APPPAH)** www.birthpsychology.com Articles, research

~ **Birth International** www.birthinternational.com Childbirth educator Andrea Robertson's website, resources for parents and practitioners

~ **Birth Resource Centre** www.birthresourcecentre.org.uk (Edinburgh, UK) Support and information for parents, newsletter, library, classes, groups, homebirth support

~ **Birthworks International** www.birthworks.org (US) Support and information for parents, articles, classes

~ **European Network of Childbirth Associations** www.enca.eu Support and information for parents, listings in 16 countries across Europe

~ **Fathers To Be** www.fatherstobe.org Support and information for expectant and new fathers

~ **Gentle Birth, Gentle Mothering** www.sarahjbuckley.com Author Sarah Buckley's website, articles, talks for parents and practitioners

~ **Primal Health** www.primalhealthresearch.com, www.wombecology.com Michel Odent's primal health database, articles, essays, conferences

Breastfeeding

~ **Association of Breastfeeding Mothers** www.abm.me.uk National UK counselling hotline 08444-1122-949 (9.30am-10.30pm)

~ **Baby Milk Action** www.babymilkaction.org Campaigning group

~ **Biological Nurturing** www.biologicalnurturing.com Suzanne Colson's mother-centred approach to breastfeeding, articles, resources, conferences

~ **Breastfeeding Network** www.breastfeedingnetwork.org.uk National UK supporterline 0844-412-4664 (9.30am-9.30pm)

~ **Breastfeeding Online** www.breastfeedingonline.com Useful articles

~ **La Leche League International**
UK resources: www.laleche.org.uk National UK helpline
0845-120-2918 (urgent calls only through night)
Worldwide support contacts and information:
www.llli.org

~ **NCT Breastfeeding Line** www.nct.org.uk
UK counsellors 0870-444-8708 (8am-10pm)

~ **Righard L MD,** *Delivery Self-Attachment* DVD
(LOS ANGELES: GEDDES PRODUCTIONS, 1995/2005)
www.geddesproductions.com

Cranial Osteopathy and Craniosacral Therapy

~ **Bethan Elsdale** UKCP CSTA, Craniosacral Therapist
(Edinburgh, UK) www.bethan-elsdale.co.uk,
Bethan@Bethan-Elsdale.co.uk 0131-555-1836

~ **Donald Howitt** Cranial Osteopath (Edinburgh, UK)
donald@cspt.co.uk 0131-446-9872

~ **Lindsay Campbell** Osteopath (Glasgow, UK)
0141-571-7911

~ **The Craniosacral Therapy Association of the UK (CSTA)**
www.craniosacral.co.uk

~ **General Osteopathic Council**
www.osteopathy.org.uk

Doulas

~ **Birth Companions** www.birthcompanions.org.uk
Doulas working with women in UK prisons

~ **Doula Australia** www.doula.org.au or bellybelly.com.au
Doula community in Australia, listings, courses

~ **Doula Association of Ireland** www.doulaassociation
ofireland.com Doulas working in the Republic of Ireland

~ **DONA (Doulas of North America) International**
www.dona.org US-based association for doulas around the
world, training, certification, publications and resources

~ **Doula UK** www.doula.org.uk National organisation for UK
doulas, listings, doula courses, assessment/mentorship for new
doulas (Recognition Process), hardship fund, gift voucher
scheme

~ **European Doulas' Project** www.doulas.info/europemap.php
Listings of doula networks in 19 European countries

~ **Scottish Doula Network** www.scottishdoulanetwork.co.uk
Doulas working in Scotland, Cumbria and Northumberland
(UK), doula courses

Emotional Support

POSTNATAL DEPRESSION

~ **Association for Post Natal Illness** (APNI) www.apni.org
(UK) Helpline 020-7386-0868 (10am-2pm) Support, resources

~ **MAMA** (Meet a Mum Association) www.mama.co.uk
Helpline 0845-120-3746 (7pm-10pm) UK peer support

~ **Postpartum Support International** www.postpartum.net
(US/International) Helpline 800-944-4773 Resources,
education, research

BIRTH TRAUMA

~ **Birth Trauma Association** www.birthtraumaassociation.
org.uk (UK) Support: support@birthtraumaassociation.org.uk

~ **Sheila Kitzinger's Birth Crisis** www.sheilakitzinger.com/
BirthCrisis.htm (UK) 01865-300266 Regional helplines,
workshops, resources

COUNSELLING AND BIRTH PROCESS

~ **Bethan Elsdale** UKCP CSTA, Core Process Psychotherapy
(Edinburgh, UK) www.bethan-elsdale.co.uk 0131-555-1836

~ **Charisse Basquin**, Early Imprints (Scotland, UK)
earlyimprints@btinternet.com 01333-450-302

~ **Kathy Williams**, counselling/psychotherapy
  (Edinburgh, UK) 01968-672-698

~ **Leonie Buchan**, humanistic counselling
  (Glasgow, UK) 0141-946 9764

~ **British Association for Counselling and Psychotherapy**
  (BACP) www.bapc.co.uk

~ **UK Council for Psychotherapy** (UKCP) www.ukcp.org.uk

Health and Physical Wellbeing

AQUANATAL

~ ask your midwife, doula or at your local swimming pool

BABY MASSAGE

~ ask your health visitor, midwife or doula for local classes

BIRTH PREPARATION and/or
POSTNATAL SUPPORT

~ **Birthing from Within** www.birthingfromwithin.com (US)

~ **International College of Spiritual Midwifery**
  www.womenofspirit.asn.au (Aus)

~ **Lamaze International** www.lamaze.org (US/International)

~ **National Childbirth Trust** (NCT) www.nct.org.uk (UK)

YOGA, INCLUDING BIRTH PREPARATION and/or
POSTNATAL SUPPORT:

~ **Active Birth Centre** www.activebirthcentre.com (UK)

~ **Birth Connections** www.birthconnections.co.uk
  (Glasgow, UK)

~ **Birth Resource Centre** www.birthresourcecentre.co.uk
  (Edinburgh, UK)

OPTIMAL FETAL POSITIONING

~ Spinning Babies www.spinningbabies.com
  Resources for parents

VBAC

~ **VBAC Support** www.vbac.com (US) Resources for parents
  and practitioners

~ **Caesarean Birth and VBAC Information**
  www.caesarean.org.uk (UK) Articles

~ **Darlington T and G,** *The Birth of Aasha* DVD (2006)
  www.garfielddarlington.com

HOMEBIRTH AND WATERBIRTH

~ **Homebirth** www.homebirth.org.uk Support, home breech
  and waterbirth stories

~ **Waterbirth International** www.waterbirth.org Resources, articles

Homeopathy

HOMEOPATHS

~ **Adela Stockton** MA, DIHom (Scotland, UK)
www.birthconsultancy.org

~ **Lyssa Clayton** Dip Hom Ed, ECH (Edinburgh, UK)
lyssa.clayton@yahoo.co.uk 0131 447 3248 or 07906 312 332

~ **Rebecca Preston** RSHom, PCH (Edinburgh, UK)
www.scothomeopathy.com 0131-556-1536

~ **Dr Gabriel Blass** BSc, MBChB, RSHom (Glasgow, UK)
www.homeopathy-glasgow.co.uk

HOMEOPATHIC PHARMACY:

~ **Helios Homeopathic Pharmacy** www.helios.co.uk Remedies (mail order), homeopathic packs (childbirth, first aid, travel), advice, literature, resources

~ **British Homeopathic Association and Homeopathic Trust** www.trusthomeopathy.org

~ **Society of Homeopaths** www.homeopathy-soh.org

~ **The Homeopathic Medical Association** www.the-hma.org

Immunisation

~ **Justice Awareness and Basic Support** www.jabs.org.uk
UK-based peer support for parents, information, research

~ **The Informed Parent** www.informedparent.com Resources
for parents

~ **What Doctors Don't Tell You** www.wddty.co.uk
Information, research, literature

Massage for Pregnancy

~ **Alison Gean Davies** MA, PMAS, Pre and Perinatal Massage
(Scotland, UK) Amca.gean@tiscali.co.uk 01786-823650

~ **Isabel Park**, Certified Maternity Massage Therapist (Glasgow,
UK) IsabelPark@phonecoop.coop 0141-942-5806

Midwives

~ **Ina May Gaskin** www.inamay.com US traditional midwife,
author, activist, innovator

~ **Independent Midwives Association**
www.independentmidwives.org.uk UK regional contacts

~ **Mary Cronk** et al www.sharingtheskills.co.uk UK independent midwife, specialist in breech birth, twins and other
unusual normal births

~ **Midwifery Today** www.midwiferytoday.com US midwifery network, publications, communications, conferences

~ **Radical Midwives Association** www.radmid.demon.co.uk UK regional contacts

~ **Sara Wickham** www.withwoman.co.uk UK independent midwife, essential articles, links with The Farm

~ **Scotbirth** www.scotbirth.co.uk Independent midwives in Scotland

~ **The Farm Midwives** www.thefarm.org US traditional midwifery centre founded by Ina May Gaskin, birth/postnatal services, practitioner workshops

Spiritual Birth

~ **International College of Spiritual Midwifery** www.womenofspirit.asn.au (Aus) Workshops, gatherings, resources and retreats for parents and practitioners

~ **Sacred Birthing** www.sacredbirthing.com Conscious birth and parenting resources

When a Baby Dies

~ **Miscarriage Association** www.miscarriageassociation.org.uk (UK) Helpline 01924-200799 (9am-4pm)

~ **Stillbirth and Neonatal Death Society** (SANDS) www.uk-sands.org National UK helpline 020-7436-5881

(9.30am-5.30pm) or helpline@uk-sands.org Support for anyone affected by the death of a baby – UK regional contacts

Acknowledgments

My heartfelt thanks go to Nadine Edwards, Lyssa Clayton, Miranda Page and Lesley Ann Patrick for their valuable insight to my writings, also to all the mothers, fathers, midwives and doulas who shared their stories with me for this book, and to all those whose births I have been privileged to attend. Most of all I thank my daughter Marly for teaching me what gentle birth is from the inside out, and my husband Matt Baker for being so patient yet brutally honest when I needed it.

FINDHORN PRESS

Books, Card Sets,
CDs & DVDs
that inspire and uplift

For a complete catalogue,
please contact:

Findhorn Press Ltd
305a The Park, Findhorn
Forres IV36 3TE
Scotland, UK

Telephone
+44-(0)1309-690582
Fax
+44-(0)131-777-2711
eMail
info@findhornpress.com

or consult our catalogue online
(with secure order facility) on
www.findhornpress.com

For information on the Findhorn Foundation:
www.findhorn.org